Dyslexia:
F*ckine Deal With It!

Andy Webb

ISBN: 9781527238428

First published 2020

Contents

Chapter 1:
He Won't Amount To Much

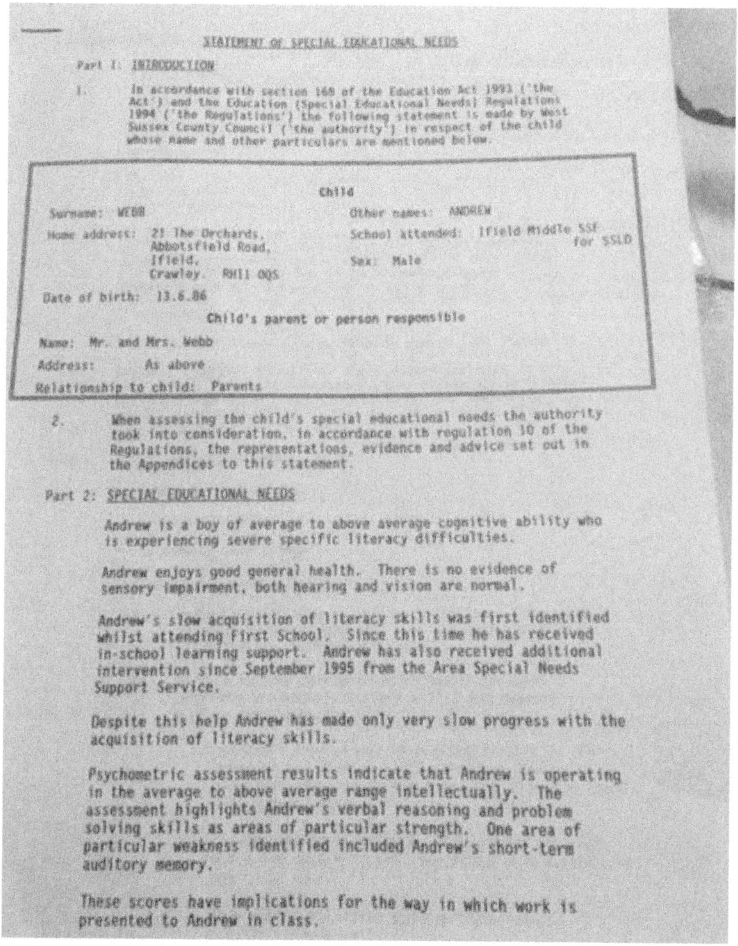

STATEMENT OF SPECIAL EDUCATIONAL NEEDS

Part 1: INTRODUCTION

1. In accordance with section 168 of the Education Act 1993 ('the Act') and the Education (Special Educational Needs) Regulations 1994 ('the Regulations') the following statement is made by West Sussex County Council ('the authority') in respect of the child whose name and other particulars are mentioned below.

Child

Surname: WEBB

Other names: ANDREW

Home address: 21 The Orchards, Abbotsfield Road, Ifield, Crawley. RH11 0QS

School attended: Ifield Middle SSF for SSLD

Sex: Male

Date of birth: 13.6.86

Child's parent or person responsible

Name: Mr. and Mrs. Webb

Address: As above

Relationship to child: Parents

2. When assessing the child's special educational needs the authority took into consideration, in accordance with regulation 10 of the Regulations, the representations, evidence and advice set out in the Appendices to this statement.

Part 2: SPECIAL EDUCATIONAL NEEDS

Andrew is a boy of average to above average cognitive ability who is experiencing severe specific literacy difficulties.

Andrew enjoys good general health. There is no evidence of sensory impairment, both hearing and vision are normal.

Andrew's slow acquisition of literacy skills was first identified whilst attending First School. Since this time he has received in-school learning support. Andrew has also received additional intervention since September 1995 from the Area Special Needs Support Service.

Despite this help Andrew has made only very slow progress with the acquisition of literacy skills.

Psychometric assessment results indicate that Andrew is operating in the average to above average range intellectually. The assessment highlights Andrew's verbal reasoning and problem solving skills as areas of particular strength. One area of particular weakness identified included Andrew's short-term auditory memory.

These scores have implications for the way in which work is presented to Andrew in class.

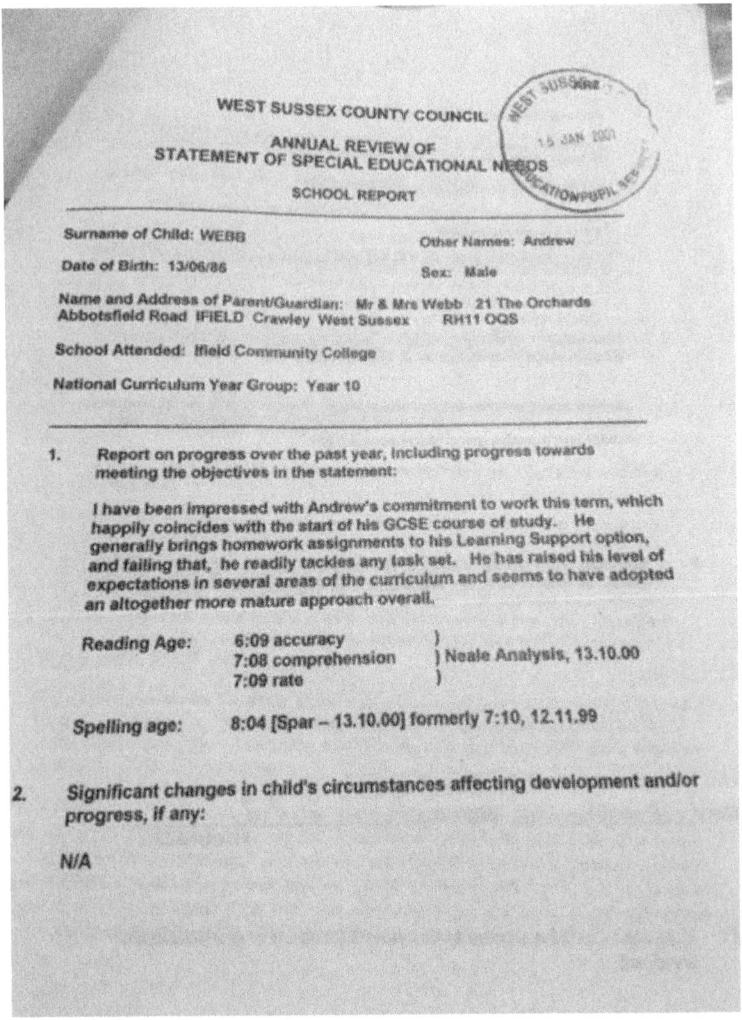

WEST SUSSEX COUNTY COUNCIL

ANNUAL REVIEW OF
STATEMENT OF SPECIAL EDUCATIONAL NEEDS

SCHOOL REPORT

Surname of Child: WEBB
Other Names: Andrew

Date of Birth: 13/06/86
Sex: Male

Name and Address of Parent/Guardian: Mr & Mrs Webb 21 The Orchards Abbotsfield Road IFIELD Crawley West Sussex RH11 OQS

School Attended: Ifield Community College

National Curriculum Year Group: Year 10

1. Report on progress over the past year, including progress towards meeting the objectives in the statement:

I have been impressed with Andrew's commitment to work this term, which happily coincides with the start of his GCSE course of study. He generally brings homework assignments to his Learning Support option, and failing that, he readily tackles any task set. He has raised his level of expectations in several areas of the curriculum and seems to have adopted an altogether more mature approach overall.

Reading Age: 6:09 accuracy; 7:08 comprehension; 7:09 rate } Neale Analysis, 13.10.00

Spelling age: 8:04 [Spar – 13.10.00] formerly 7:10, 12.11.99

2. Significant changes in child's circumstances affecting development and/or progress, if any:

N/A

Andrew Webb (13.6.86)

Andrew's literacy skills were tested on the Wechsler Objective Reading Dimensions giving results for reading, reading comprehension and spelling which were at or below the 2nd percentile.

The testing of Basic Number Skills which includes sums involving the four rules and numbers to 100, Andrew scored at the 4th percentile.

The results for literacy and numeracy indicate some highly significant differences between Andrew's cognitive ability and his literacy and mathematical attainments.

At school Andrew is described as shy and sensitive, already showing concern about secondary transfer. He has developed a range of strategies for coping with his learning difficulties. His approaches give him some level of independence within the classroom setting. Andrew's oral skills are good. He is generally well informed and makes a useful contribution to class discussions.

Andrew is described as very agile being good at P.E. and sports.

Andrew's literacy difficulties are so significant that he will need special help at his secondary school to enable him to access the curriculum and will benefit from being in a school with special support facilities for pupils with severe specific literacy difficulties.

Part 3: SPECIAL EDUCATIONAL PROVISION

A. Educational Objectives

To gain functional literacy and numeracy skills.

To enhance self esteem.

B. Special Educational Provision

1. Andrew will be able to follow the National Curriculum in an ordinary school but will need the work modified to allow for his learning difficulties.

2. He will need to follow an individually designed programme to develop literacy skills and numeracy skills, which aims to:

   - develop a broad range of reading strategies where decoding and phonic skills should be taught in parallel with word recognition, use should be made of mnemonic memory aids

   - give access to structured, interesting material where new vocabulary is introduced in a controlled way

   - give opportunities to work on rhyme and alliteration activities

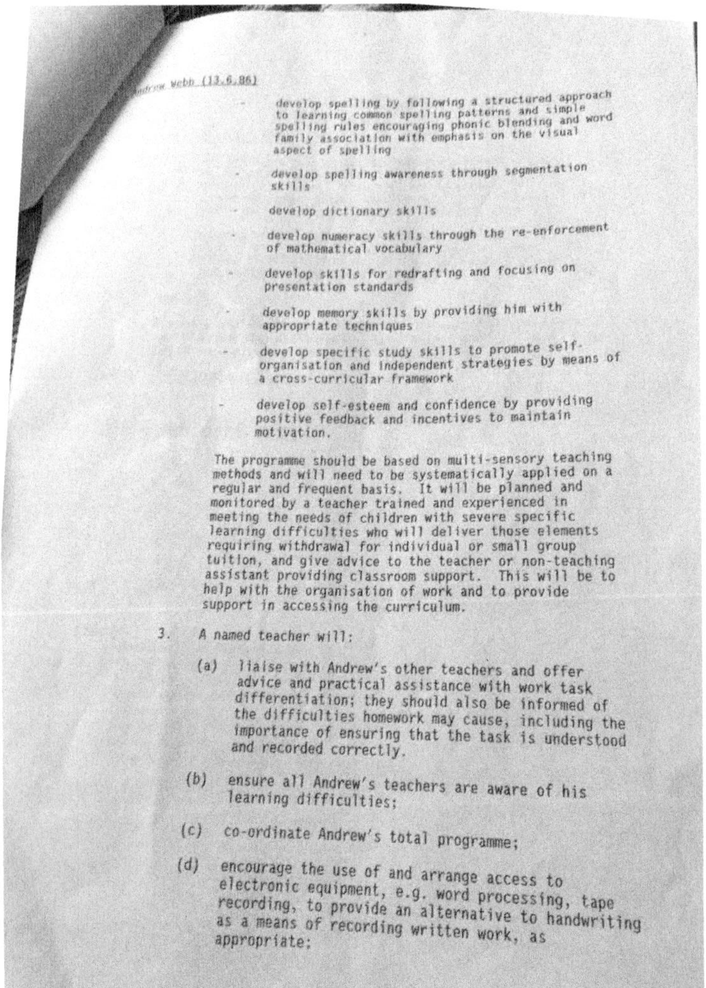

ndrew Webb (13.6.86)

- develop spelling by following a structured approach to learning common spelling patterns and simple spelling rules encouraging phonic blending and word family association with emphasis on the visual aspect of spelling
- develop spelling awareness through segmentation skills
- develop dictionary skills
- develop numeracy skills through the re-enforcement of mathematical vocabulary
- develop skills for redrafting and focusing on presentation standards
- develop memory skills by providing him with appropriate techniques
- develop specific study skills to promote self-organisation and independent strategies by means of a cross-curricular framework
- develop self-esteem and confidence by providing positive feedback and incentives to maintain motivation.

The programme should be based on multi-sensory teaching methods and will need to be systematically applied on a regular and frequent basis. It will be planned and monitored by a teacher trained and experienced in meeting the needs of children with severe specific learning difficulties who will deliver those elements requiring withdrawal for individual or small group tuition, and give advice to the teacher or non-teaching assistant providing classroom support. This will be to help with the organisation of work and to provide support in accessing the curriculum.

3. A named teacher will:

(a) liaise with Andrew's other teachers and offer advice and practical assistance with work task differentiation; they should also be informed of the difficulties homework may cause, including the importance of ensuring that the task is understood and recorded correctly.

(b) ensure all Andrew's teachers are aware of his learning difficulties;

(c) co-ordinate Andrew's total programme;

(d) encourage the use of and arrange access to electronic equipment, e.g. word processing, tape recording, to provide an alternative to handwriting as a means of recording written work, as appropriate;

Andrew WEBB (13.6.86)

2.

when trying to work out unknown words. He achieved a score which places him on the 2nd centile for this task. This means that for a hundred children of a similar age to Andrew 98 would be expected to score the same or better. This gives Andrew a basic reading age equivalent of 7.00 years (age at testing 11.11 years). Whilst Andrew's basic reading skills do remain significantly delayed it is important to acknowledge that he now takes a much more positive and structured approach to reading unknown words.

On the spelling task Andrew had to write from dictation a number of words that I gave him, placing them in a sentence to provide him with a context. Again Andrew showed evidence of a basic spelling vocabulary. He also demonstrated that he has learned some common letter strings which, for instance, allowed him to correctly write the word "right." Andrew showed some awareness that he had made errors and did on occasion try to self-correct although he was not always happy with his final response. He will continue to need a good deal of work to help him develop a more systematic approach to spelling unknown words and thus at the moment some of his spellings might be a little difficult to read even within context eg

for "eight" he wrote "haret"
for "counting" he wrote "caninter"
for "picture" he wrote "piceter"

He achieved a score which places him on the 1st centile for this task, giving him a spelling age of 6.09 years.

On the reading comprehension task Andrew had to read independently from a passage, the first few of which were illustrated and then answer a question about it. He worked really hard through this task and brought a range of skills to the task that meant that even when he had managed to read very little of the passage he made a good attempt at answering the question. He made an attempt on 28 of the passages and I discontinued the task slightly early as I wanted him to feel a sense of achievement about what he had done. He achieved a score which places him on the 4th centile for this task giving him a reading comprehension age equivalent of 8.00 years.

It is possible to combine the above scores to provide a global view of the development of Andrew's literacy skills. When this is done he achieves a score which places him on the 1st centile indicating that he is continuing to experience very significant difficulties with the development of his literacy skills.

In talking with Andrew he did say that he feels he is beginning to "understand things more." He told me that he feels he does try hard at school but that at the same time he can have "moods about what I am doing." Andrew indicated that he does enjoy PE, practical activities and Drama at school. He also told me that he does like people and that he will try to solve some of his own problems if he can. He explained to me that he is aware that he has difficulties with English and he also felt that he has problems in Mathematics.

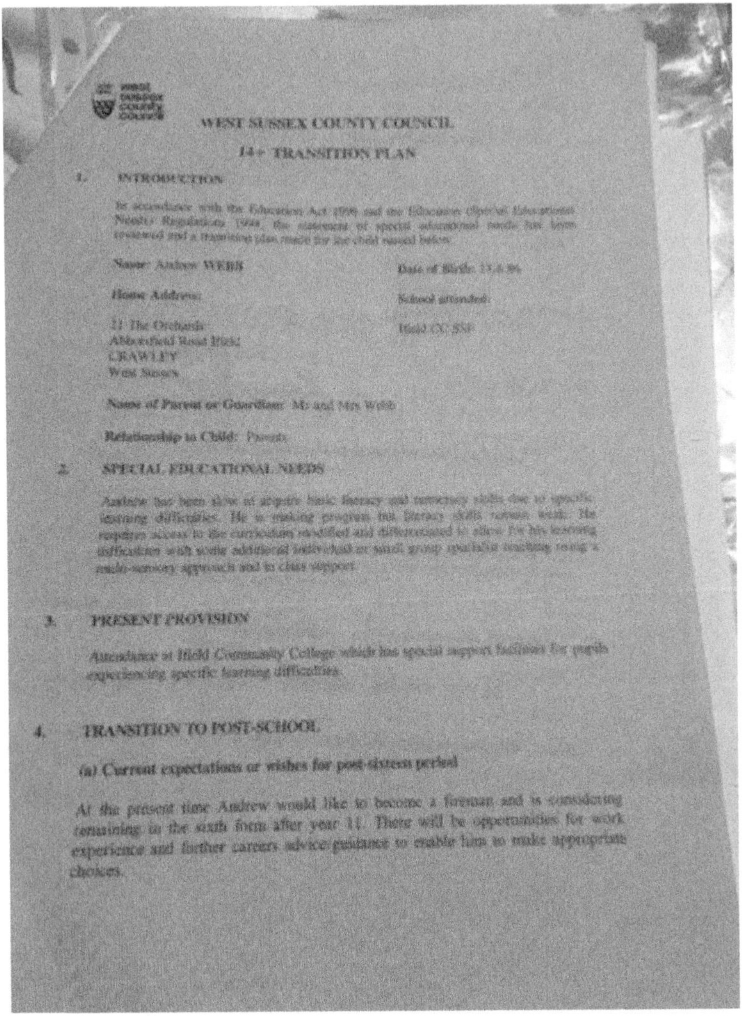

WEST SUSSEX COUNTY COUNCIL

14+ TRANSITION PLAN

1. INTRODUCTION

In accordance with the Education Act 1996 and the Education (Special Educational Needs) Regulations 1994, the statement of special educational needs has been reviewed and a transition plan made for the child named below.

Name: Andrew WEBB

Date of Birth: [illegible]

Home Address:

11 The Orchards
Abbotsfield Road Ifield
CRAWLEY
West Sussex

School attended:

Ifield CC SSF

Name of Parent or Guardian: Mr and Mrs Webb

Relationship to Child: Parents

2. SPECIAL EDUCATIONAL NEEDS

Andrew has been slow to acquire basic literacy and numeracy skills due to specific learning difficulties. He is making progress but literacy skills remain weak. He requires access to the curriculum modified and differentiated to allow for his learning difficulties with some additional individual or small group specialist teaching using a multi-sensory approach and in class support.

3. PRESENT PROVISION

Attendance at Ifield Community College which has special support facilities for pupils experiencing specific learning difficulties.

4. TRANSITION TO POST-SCHOOL

(a) Current expectations or wishes for post-sixteen period

At the present time Andrew would like to become a fireman and is considering remaining in the sixth form after year 11. There will be opportunities for work experience and further careers advice/guidance to enable him to make appropriate choices.

Chapter 1: He Won't Amount To Much

Wow! After reading that people you would think there is no hope for Andrew! Well think again since then I have gone on to:

- Completed a 4-year apprentice in Electrical & Mechanical Engineering
- Achieved the highest high voltage switching qualification in the rail industry
- Gone on to complete football coaching badges qualification and currently holds a UEFA B licence I have coached and worked at premier league, championship football club also worked in Holland, Italy and Spain.
- Worked for one of the biggest airports in the world as an electrical mechanical engineer
- Worked at West Sussex Fire and Rescue Service
- Entered bodybuilding physiques competitions
- Presented seminars on stage to 100s of people
- A Director of AW Rail Network system limited which has worked on some of the biggest re development project in the rail industries history.

So not bad for someone in the 2nd per centile (by the way which I thought was good at the time ha ha) with a reading age of 7 years old at 12 years old and 6 year olds spelling that's half my age.

Hi I'm Andrew Webb and first thing first - a few disclaimers and the reason for this book before you use it as a doorstop or as a coffee stand (there was a lot of coffee that help me to write this book - great stuff). Disclaimers:

1. This book is a little err … different ;
2. I swear a bit in the book - I swear in real life a lot ;
3. I may offend friend's, family and people I love if so sorry don't read ha-ha;
4. People who are not patience and understanding shouldn't read this – its a book about dyslexia not war and bloody peace!

RIGHT ! the reason I wrote this book - have you ever wonder why your friends, family, children, boyfriend, girlfriend, co-workers, players you coach or people on the street do certain things a way or seem to not get what you're saying or doing? Well maybe they're dyslexic? Or you yourself not understand why you're not getting things when everyone around you does? Maybe you're dyslexic and you don't even know it!

What if I told you that this book had the potential to change your life for the better- would you prick your ears up and listen? Over the last few years my life has change and I've seen so many people feel ashamed, upset, frustrated with no self-confident been afraid at their struggle with day to day tasks and not living dreams due to social, education ,self-image and lack of understanding. I believe that every person has the right to at least try to do what there want in life or have a go at it, succeed or fail at whatever it is. To see the change in someone life just by understanding what they don't get by being showed a different way can make a huge and important change to their life and everyone around them as well. In this book I will give you:

- A view Inside the world of the dyslexic person
- Success stories of dyslexic people via interviews detailing their life experiences
- The routines, habits, tactics and skills to help you get through day to day struggles that normal people (what is normal by the way) take for granted
- The machine of the brain of dyslexia (fuck neuro science stuff I got a E in science)
- Hopefully on this journey things that will make you laugh - because you got to laugh as life too short to waste or worry people.

Other reason I wrote this book is for ME- YES ME! I've always been a person if told "you can't do that" then you're fucked because this stupid hairy man - billy big balls here will just go do/ try it just to piss you off ha-ha-ha.

No really if I could just help one person realise their potential or help them tap into the reason for their struggle then this book will be worth the hours of me wanting to throw the laptop up the wall and shout at it like an idiotic character from some Danny Dyer tough nut film ha-ha. To show that you can do whatever you want in this world if you just go for it and some way somehow you'll get there.

LASTLY the biggest reason for all of this for me is my inspiration in life that my little boy Harry ever since the day I saw my beautiful long orangutan in the hospital he changed my life for the better and every single thing I go onto to do is because of him so I love you my little monkey.

Dyslexia facts %

You'll be thinking WHAT are you doing I hate maths and you throw this in the first chapter you smash it at me cheers - but look at the facts .

- Overall 53% of 2029 prisoners at Chelmsford were diagnosed as dyslexic compared to 10% of UK population (British Dyslexics Association)
- 1/25 people in the world are dyslexic.
- 35% of the world entrepreneurs - are dyslexic.
- 40% of the self-made millionaire are…guess what - dyslexic;

- And listen to this 1/2 of NASA rocket scientist are dyslexic!

People with dyslexia have had exceptional vocational success in 5 key areas:

- Entrepreneurship
- Engineering
- Architecture
- Arts
- sport

Could you imagine for a second if you could - if the system helped say 20% of these prisoners into these key areas what a different society we could have. Don't get me wrong – if you are a knob you're a knob and if they deserve to be there fine I'm not some prisoner social justice carer - but from a young age some of these people have been left and failed by the system and gone down the only path they felt they could succeed or pass in! Please just read what the international definition of dyslexia association states:

"DYSLEXIA is a specific learning disability that is neurological in origin it is characterized by difficulties with accurate and or fluent word recognition and poor spelling and decoding abilities these difficulties typically results from a deficit in the phonological component of language that is often unexpected in relation to

other cognitive abilities and the provision of effective classroom instruction secondary consequences **may include problem's in reading comprehension and reduced reading experience that** impede **growth of vocabulary and background knowledge "**

When reading this you can see the highlight words that how dyslexia is seen by the world as a disability - what chance do dyslexics have?

"life is short and you've got to get the most out of it"

Gwen Stefani songwriter fashion designer actress

Information and fact to help you as an adult, child, coach, teacher or parents to spot the signs of dyslexia if some of these relate to you and you have not been tested or slip through the gap as a lots of people have! I have put information in the book about how and where you can go to get more information and/ or where you can have an assessment.

- Dyslexia is genetic : simple as that you - can't catch it or develop it of cure it. I've had people try to tell me what it is - but it comes from your family tree. There is a 50% chance you can have it if one of your parents have it or a 25% chance if one of your grandparents has it.
- The brain is wired differently: as I will go into more through the book.
- You can't process language formats: for example you can't see from someone text or writing the mood/emotion or understand the importance of a situation in written form.
- Directionality: so for examples you can't understand words getting confused before –after, next-pervious, first –last, over-under, yesterday -tomorrow and days of the week.
- Time: no concept of time and action i.e. when to leave to go to work, gauge time to get somewhere i.e. trains time, kick off times and dates so being late is not good but maybe if a child is late to college or work - then maybe you can help .

- Memory function: its difficult to follow a chain of instructions some one with dyslexia needs "jobs" broken down into sequencing and processes - like shopping list, locking doors, cooking, pick-ups, tasks and cleaning all in one go is too much to process.
- Random information: moving house and remembering addresses, post codes, door numbers, i.e. got to 7 Crawley Street which is RH11 2FE instead of 17 Crawley Avenue RH11 3EF
- The following are signs of dyslexia in adults that can be easily missed – do any of these ring true for you? .
- Got solids results at school Ds but had to work twice as hard as everyone else.
- Very slow reader or trying to get out of reading with kid's, family, friends and at work.
- Can't use a spell checker or a dictionary as a waste of time as you have get a word close to it and then try to read 25 other words that are close to it!
- Can't learn foreign language speaking is ok but written no chance.
- Confusing left and right - I spend my life putting Harry's shoes on the wrong feet he knows and tells me off!!

"I'd try to concentrate on what I was reading then I'd get to the end of the page and have very little memory of anything I'd read"

Tom cruise

Chapter 2:
Early days

I'm not going to start going into some kind of Michael Aspel style red book this is your life auto bio (young people there's a lot of throw backs in this book look them up). As you're not going to care - but what I want to do is to give you a snap shot of my school's days and maybe something you will see will help you or your child in their or your life at some point.

I had a great childhood at home I'm the youngest of five kids Mum and Dad came from London. I loved going up to London with my Dad, he used to work at Ready-Mix as a crane driver in Wandsworth Bridge or I would go with my Mum to Gatwick Airport to help give people their tickets for holiday sitting behind a checking desk – My Mum used to work for Britannia. I loved it all the girls used to look after me in the back and buy my McDonalds - how funny now to think you could do all that with the security now! Also weird to think that I fixed the same checking desk as a part of my role as an engineer at the airport.

I would go to my Nan and Grandad's in Lavender Hill I remember days being with my brother sisters and cousin's in my Nan and Grandad's dining room practicing some routine or play we would perform with my whole family - parents aunts and uncles all in a tiny front room smoking away eating corn beef sandwiches and tea (I hate corned beef) I used to throw mine over the back garden on to the railway track funny enough I worked later on in life on those tracks too - see you are your environment! In that front room it used to be like Matthew Kelly's Stars in Your Eyes - we would come out and we would muck the play up and shout wait 2 minutes go back and try again. I can image the west end stage was like this every mid- day Matinee!

So life was petty great! I started first school had a best friends Lloyd and Ben and a girlfriend who when your 6 you're going marry lived together forever ha ha! Playing football every day this is a great montage of happiness then…Bang all of a sudden I remember being in a class in last year before moving schools (I started school at 5 – long story for another book) and my teacher saying "right we are going to all read this book and we going to do a test after see what you pick up" my world changed right then, .my peers would have their heads down all happy in silence writing away and for me it was blank nothing I look down at the page and see:

Thew ord sare n otsp aced cor rect ly

We spell wrds xatle az tha snd to us.

Somtimsallthelettersarepushedtogther

Aa Bb Cc Dd Ee
Ff Gg Hh Ii Jj Kk
Ll Mm Nn Oo Pp
Qq Rr Ss Tt Uu
Vv Ww Xx Yy Zz

and after an hour the teacher would go around checking and testing and I would have nothing so day one I failed, day two I failed day three I failed... this went on for months and then years. I remember my Mum coming to parents evening and the teacher saying "Andrew's a lovely, nice boy but his not interested doesn't want to write anything" my Mum even came into to school sometimes to read to a little group but again nothing. When she was in I was so happy see my Mum at school. I will always thank my Mum for not letting me go to the school next door she fought hard against the school when they told her I needed to go to Deerwood Special School for mentally retarder children with serious learning difficulty.

I transitions to middle school and I lost my girlfriend she moved away my friend Ben moved to Australia and Lloyd was still in year below in first school and now I was getting negative re-enforcement kids saying "you can't play football with us girls saying can't play kiss chase and doing the classic tongue in the bottom jaw pushing out to say I was dumb!! By the age of 9 (it doesn't matter how much personal resilience I had) I felt I was wearing this shroud of shame over me even when at school and on Sunday nights feeling so anxious, upset and worried about going to school my Mum knew I had changed. Her happy little son was now a shadow of myself only time I was happy was football training and football matches on a Sunday morning .

So in my last year and bit of before secondly school my Mum push and push and got me tested for learning difficulties. I still remember funnily enough (memory's for dyslexic is not great!) but these experiences stick and the women with the old giant stop clock (see the report above) my Mum and Dad sat me down and told me that I have DYSLEXIA "I ask am I going to die? My Mum said "no darling its going just take you a little longer to do stuff" My world lighten up and the doors open to learning when I met this amazing women her name was Mrs Highly .

I would leave my class as see her in this small room with about 5 or 6 other kids and she would say we going to write a story about your weekend or about history she would say tell me explain and I will write - it was brilliant! We would do maths and she would use my love of football to engage me i.e. 3+3 = 6 so Chelsea with blue bricks man united red bricks how many goals did each team score? I would read fuzz buzz books and she would tell me how great my effort was. We would act out history or draw it and I would watch TV with my Dad and he would tell me about history and test me - he would say there will be 10 question in whatever we were watching. He would tell me Arsenal scored 6 so can you beat this and he would read the question and I would answer. My school life was starting to become a little better. In the last year at school I made the football team and played upfront and scored a lot of goals which with the other lads like so I played with them in the breaks so life was easier.

The next unhappy phase happen when I went to secondly school. So now at 12 years old I would be sitting in English class and the teachers would say we are going to read a chapter each starting from left table to the right and we will read 5 chapters. As someone would stand up and stared reading I would begin to get that same red fear feeling myself heat up like a ready break child advert panicking - my heart beating through my chest I would be trying to work out if I would be in that number counting the heads on the table then in if it was me I would ask people behind me to switch chairs trying find a way out! My turn was getting close and those awful words "Mr Webb stand up" I wouldn't know were we were in the book as I been doing my upmost to get away from this as I stood up so nervous, my hands shanking I would look at the page and it would just be a blur. I could hear kids sniggering to each other as I would attempt it but the words wouldn't come out and sweat would be dripping from my head ,the teacher would then start getting annoyed to get on with it., I would say I can't read it and she really annoyed then telling me to stop mucking about get on with it as I was holding the class up! I would try again - then depending on the teacher I either be sent out for pissing about or told sit down as I did this I could hear other laughing saying in the background he's odd he's 12 and can't read what a retard! I would drop into my seat and feel embarrassed and humiliated. It was like this until the last year of secondly school. Some teachers just didn't get it or understand. I thought I was doomed to fail.

Then as puberty kicked in (going to bed one night to waking up with ripped pyjamas - muscle and a shit load of hair like teen wolf!) I became to understand what I was good at and what I was not good at. It was then that I did my work experience at Gatwick Airport Fire and Rescue with my friend Lloyds Dad Ian Denmen., I knew in those two weeks that all I wanted to do if I could was to play football and be a firefighter. I wasn't willing to be average and I set my mind to making money and creating a better life for my self than was expected of me. I changed my mind-set from "I cant to I have to do well at my GCSE" I needed to do well to get a chance to apply to get in to the fire service and Ian told me and all firefighters qualify in a trade he said "mate be a bricklayer electrical plumber or Engineering". DING, DING, DING that in the list above of skills that people with Dyslexia excel at.

Chapter 2: Early days

To be honest the "support unit" as they called it in secondary school wasn't that good. I would be in there and I felt like Jack Nicholson in one flew over cuckoo nest or Leo DiCaprio in shutter island - I knew something was different about how I was and how tough it was for some of the other.You had kids trying to take their clothes off or hiding in cupboards or punching walls or fighting each other or just running up and down tables!, Not really somewhere you could learn! I did have one lovely lady and I am gutted that I can't remember her name but she started coming to classes instead and would sit with me. Learning was brilliant again I could listen take part and she would write what I was saying in a way I would understand it. She really did help me build confidence and I just want to say thank you to this lady. She will never know how much she helped me! We would have a chat about the weekend I never felt dumb when I spoke to her and she smelt really good all the time and used to dress very stylishly .

Towards the end of school life I felt I had out grown of school it wasn't for me and I hated it really but I knew that I didn't want to sit down the shops or bike sheds smoking gear, drugs or even playing football at lunch time . I knew if I wanted nice things and to help my family and have a good life that I needed to stay away from this at school and try concentrate on getting the best results I could get.

Results day came and I did well - I was happy I had achieved something I never thought I could. I decided to enrol in college.

College was for me I loved it and I was good at it! The lecturers were real they treated you like men and women and took the piss out of you (in a good way) being with older people really help me. This is one of my first tips to you - Have no SHAME just put yourself out there, so what if you fail, fuck up or get rejected or someone say no! It doesn't really matter in the end because if you keep at it and put yourself out there then opportunities will present themselves you. My first year everyone was a apprentice apart from me I had to pay for all my own books and equipment, I got a evening job in a warehouse and my Dad help pay for overalls and boots.

A man called Paul Kendell came to the college - he used to check on his apprentices for a company called Johnson Sweepers every week. I would say to him "Hi Paul, are you taking anyone on?" Paul would say "no not this year". The next week "Hi Paul, do you know when you may take apprentice on ?" He would say "No Andy I don't know some time next year" the next week "Hi Paul, look at my toolmaking jobs and welding work any news on taking anyone on?" He said "No Andy but that good work" I said " you can take it back with you if you like". This continued for a least 6 months when one day I said "Hi Paul" and he said "Andy I got you an application form and an interview booked in for you at Johnson Sweepers can you make it?" "Oh yes of course" I said and I went and I got a 4 years apprentice what I am saying is this keep trying it doesn't matter what age you are where you're from you just have the balls (or ovaries) to just keep asking keep knocking on the door, volunteer what ever it takes and it will come.

"Life takes on meaning when you become motivated set goals and charge after them in an unstoppable manner"

Les brown : motivational speaker @lesbrown77

Chapter 3:

Machines of the brain - neuro science

Let me start by saying that NO I'm not a neuro scientist and I may get somethings wrong! This is not going to turn into some terminator style T1000 idea or blow your minds - I hope that I can explain this in the best possible way so that those with dyslexia and those without can start to understand how the brain operates. By the end of this chapter you will understand how dyslexic minds function and hopefully answer a few questions for you when dealing with dyslexia.

One things that dyslexic people have in common is a cerebellar dysfunction which affects our in movements, language ,internal speech, memory and most importantly it has been proven to affect procedural learning.This was discovered by British psychologists Anglea Fawcett and Roderick Nicolson. On the following page you can see how a typical brain works while reading.

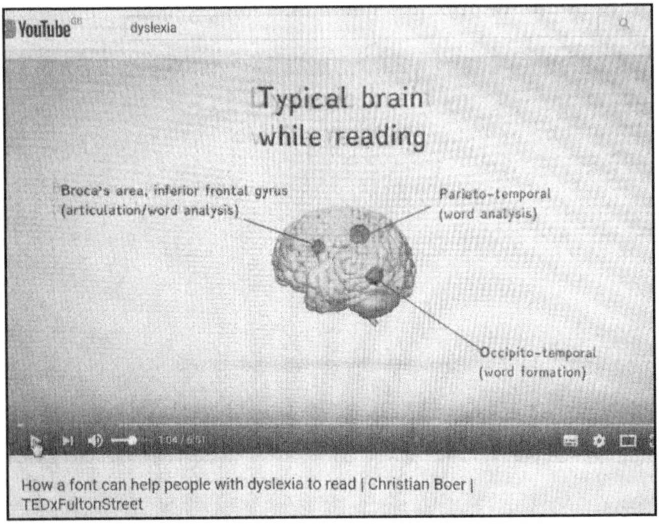

You can see that three key areas are used when scanning details on paper or information in front of us then look at the brain of a dyslexic while reading.

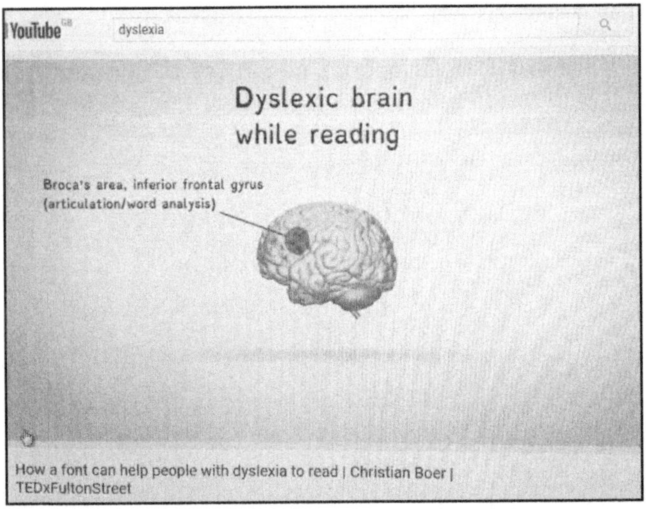

You can see that that people with dyslexia don't use the parietal temporal for word analysis and our occipital temporal for the formation of the letter and words - so before we have even started we're trying to do all three jobs just with the frontal cortex! Just image that in any other area of your life you would feel pretty knackered wouldn't you? So image that how I and others feel when trying to read. I find myself knackered if I'm on a course reading text books or reading a book of interested at home.

A little tip - when asking some with dyslexia to do something or read or study something break it down into small chunks or goals. They will still get to the same answers or achievement but just make the goals challenging but easier to achieved i.e. one page of a book or 30 min studying or 20min homework. Over the years I have had people ask me or told me "that kid doesn't get it or they are lazy after doing 10 minutes homework or two pages of a book" but this just isn't true.

The best way I can explain it is its like the start of a Formula One race - the lights go on the engines revving and the wheels spinning, the car is swishing going side by its self then...a big crash at the first corner. That's what its feel like to read or take in information in.

Your brain is not less intelligent let's get that straight! Your brain is wired differently which is a gift and this is why a dyslexic brain has a huge cognitive advantage over the average human brain - so let's delve into the neuro anatomy

Your brain has things called neurons and these neurons are interlinked to each other to send message just imagine them like an electrical cable. There are over 100 billion inside your brain which is amazing for a start! Different areas of the brain work different part of you day to day – life, emotions, reactions, communication and processing information. We have a thin layer cell that covers over the brain like a sheet call the saival cortex when this develops high cognitive skill - like increased memory, problem solving, heightened awareness and language skills. The cells are called on and organised into a functioning units which are called min columns. They are a bit like computer chips and work really well if they are talking to other mini columns in the brain around them. The distance and the scales works between these mini columns - some people will havė high density neurons (see picture below) the best way I can show you is by the cabbage is the and the toothpick are the mini columns.

Lots of short columns thin but lots group together

Other people have low density meaning less tooth picks but a lot bigger, longer and thicker

Most people will have a avenge of both and this is very important when come how you are designed and wired so if you have lots of short thin mini columns then your brain can process information with only with their neighbours because they are short and thin which means its easier due to such a high density around them to find each other i.e. see below.

The elastic bands represent electrical chemicals processing information which is less energy consuming. On the other side of the spectrum is people which low density mini columns i.e. big thick tooth picks.

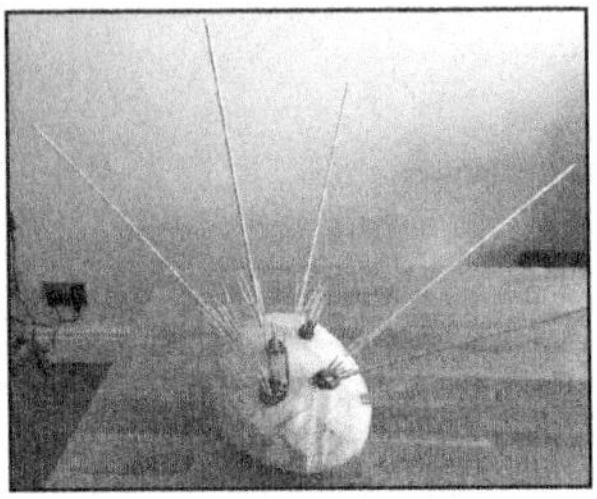

So when these single mini columns connect in to their neighbours they are accurately connecting to other parts of the brain see below.

This has an enormous impact on how information is understood. The people with short mini column are brilliant at fine details, information processing and spiral and sortation, closely related specific details highly skilled at organising tasks. Where as those with the long thick columns are not very good at these tasks. However, those with long thick columns are amazing at looking at the bigger picture, separating and understand meaningful relationships and concepts , abstract ideas and putting objects together with seemingly no connection. Often coming up with concepts whilst dreaming due to the complexity of their dream landscapes.

These brains are great at problem solving which make them very energy consuming but less efficient they can come up with new creative way of doing things i.e. those people with short columns can solve problems but only use only small area of their brain to solve it. Where as long columns use different areas of the brain and have out of the box ideas/thinking enabling them to solve problems using memory and the cognitive emotions of the brain to created the idea...guess which people are these dyslexic's...that's right (as there say in catch phase)...we are the long toothpicks! One other end of the scale - the people that have all and only short thin mini columns are autistic brains this was also discovered in the 1990s Dr Sally Shaywitz and Dr Bennett Shaywitz at Yale University in American did brain scan on people with and without dyslexia this was called functional magnetic resonance imaging for or an FMRI for short. The results showed that non-dyslexic's used the left side of the brain to learn processing activities and all dyslexics use the right side structures. We can't process pathways which cause us to look from right to left in reading or process information or details that are structured or designed. Another way explain this would be my poor fiancé Nadine - so many times she would say to ask to lock the back door or ask me to put the washing on she would tell me can you do this before you go out and do A,B,C. "Yes darling" I would say but then I be doing something and I would forgot what wash to put on or I will lock the front and forget the back or vice versa I know I have to do it but forget parts of the process even after telling me 100 times still forgetting the process that I am asked to do. I can understand why she wants to pull her hair out at times!

So if you can relate to this then you'll understand both sides. By the way I have not just given you permission not to do stuff but if you live with someone who has it then you have to understand it not because we don't care or listen it how the brain is design more of this later on in the book , right back to serious brain stuff!

With left sided people they have unbelievable skills in processing fine details, master true expertise in their field as the rights side does develop the bigger picture or details.

So wow! As you can see I have tried my best to explain what is actually going on inside the brain. Next time you're with a partner, family member, friend or the kids or your working life just think about their side of the story's or brain! Think how they see or understand things.

Below is a list of areas left sided people excel in proven by Dr Manuel Casanova of the University of Kentucky School of Medicine

Left side people without dyslexia have:

Excellent function traits like

- precision
- speed
- efficiency
- reliability
- replicability
- detailed expertise
- focus concision
- applying rules procedures
- finding primary meanings correct answers
- differences and distinctions between things
- order well organized filing cabinets style
- logical chains reasoning

Right side people with dyslexia

- see bigger picture
- spot lager context behind a situation
- multidimensionality of perspective
- new unusual connections

- inferential reasoning
- ambiguity detection
- greater mindfulness
- best fits problem solving
- spotting interesting associations relationships
- store information like murals stained glass spider web style

"The noblest pleasure is the joy of understanding"

Leonardo da Vinci

Chapter 4:
Failure

WHAT!! Right hold your horses Andy's so you start writing a book about achieving greater things in life and you stick a chapter in about failure.

Well yes and do you know why it is in this book because I have fail in every aspect of my life from school ,college, relationships being a dad (at least I feel like most of the time!) a brother, a son, a friend, a worker, a sportsman and business. However failure is the best thing that can happen to you - let me repeat this failure is the best thing that can happen to you! I fail or as I like to say "First Attempt In Life".

Four times I fail the ability test for the fire service before I pass them.

I will tell you a story - when I was 17 I went to a engineering agents. This is where there were people carrying out aptitude tests to see what area of engineering would be best for your skill set. I was excited going in but I hated exams for obvious reasons but I wanted to find out what area I may excel in. So there I was with 7 or 8 other people in the room and this bloke came in talking about the test and areas and pathways you could work in. What I noticed straight away was how this man came across I didn't like how cocky/arrogant he was.

I explained that I was dyslexic (another tip people - watch people faces when you tell them you are and see how there react towards you people change so much and you can read people real them very quickly it's a great filter for life and who you want in your life also on the flip said to this that always tell company, job interview as you are giving yourself the best change by doing this) - anyway back to the story's - so I do the test and I'm taken into a room and this bloke sit me down and say to me "look Andy your test results show that you shouldn't do engineering to be honest… you every thought about manual labour i.e. forklift drive, storemen etc." Now there is nothing wrong with this if that your role but for me this man had just try to destroy me not to help, not to support and certainly not to guide me. It was a pure no interest in helping just undermined a young man who hadn't developed the skills or self-worth just yet. I remember going home and thinking of throwing college in. My mum was scared of me failing as she love me and didn't want to get hurt she just wanted to protected me she used to say to me as I was at the kitchen table trying do course work she would say to me "don't go back to college get a full time job" but you shouldn't always listen to your parents when you're trying to find yourself in the world and your own opinion on aspects of life.

I went to my room and cried not because I was upset or afraid of failing the test but because I was being told - stop you can't do this ! I didn't understand the "no shame, fuck you" mentality just yet! But guess what about 2 years later I'm into my apprenticeship at Johnson sweepers and I'm working in the sub assembly department when my foreman comes over and say Andy can you show our new starter the ropes and guess who it was this man he didn't have no clue who I was!! I sat there laughing to myself - "yes of course I will" I said. In my head I was going to say nothing and be the better person but then I though no fuck it so I turn to him while and I asked if he remembered me? He replied "No should I?

I replied "Yes, I was the fella you told to stop engineering and become a forklift driver or manual worker" his face drop he went white and his lips try to connect together but before he could say a word I turn and said "make better choices in life mate and help people not hurt them and you may get somewhere in life". At the time I feel like it made me a better person.

(Also below is the first unedited version of this page just to show you want my grammar is like and to show you why its taken so long to bloody write this book ha-ha)

WHAT right hold your horses andys so you start wirting a book about achieving greater things in life and you stick a chatpter in about failuering well yes and do you know why its because I have fail in every apect of my life from school ,college, relationshships being a dad a brother a son a firend and a worker ,sportsmen, business, but failure is the best thing that can happen to you let me repeat this failure is the best thing that can happen to you . I fail or as I like to say F irst Attempt In Life , four times I fail abitly test for the fire service before I pass them I tell you a story when I was 17 I went to a engeering adgents in a building which is apart of wheren I lived in crawley which is the driving theory test place there where doing test to see what would be your best area of engeering to go into so I was exicted I hated exam clearly but I went finding out what area I may excel in so there was 7/8 people in the room and this blioke came in talking about the test and areas what I notice staright away was how this man came across I didn't like how cocky/argent he was so I explained that I was dyselixa also another tip people watch people faces when you tell them you are and see how there react towards you people chage so much and you can read people real them very quickly it's a greta fliter for life and who you want in your life also on the flip said to this that always always tell compamy job interview as you are not giving youself the best change by doing this anyway back to the story's so I do the testand im taken into a room and this bloke sit me down and say to me look andy you test results show that you shouldn't do enggering to be honest and you evry though about manual labour ie floklift drivering storemen now there nothink wrong with this if that your role but for me this man had just try to destroy me not to help not to support not to guide it was a pure no knowledge undermine a young man who hadn't develop the skills or self worth just I remember going home and thinking of.

I've read a book by a man called Jorden Peterson called The 12 Rule of Life. In this book he speaks about looking at you today and are you better then you were yesterday? What hit me about this was the onion concept - he says that when a layer of you dies another new layer can start to grow. This is true about failing. When you fail a part of you dies and you can either move forward and grow from it and start anew or die with it. I want you to build a mind set and change from today how you see failure because every time I have failed a new better stronger me comes alive and now I comfortable with failure. Seek out failure to achieve success in your life .

Your reading this and thinking that easier said than done when something you dream of a job, or a test you get a fail mark in - just start off little - seriously not little in term of your final goal. Learn to enjoy failing it has taken me to some amazing places in life! Look at the gym as a great example - when you're at the gym you seek to fail (work until your muscles fail) at the gym to build muscle. Failing will lead to strength and achieving great things. Never let anyone impose their negativity or worries on you. Also you have to learn to love yourself and respect others ideas but trust who you are and listen to that inner voice of yours that say I'm better than this I have something inside of me. The saying I learned over the years in engineering is that "that the man that never makes a mistake never did fuck all in the first place!"

If you don't see your future laid out in front of you or you're just floating around without a purpose then you need to strive for a purpose as humans being we excel when we have something to aim for you have to get a vision of what you want to do.

For me it's like the Greek legend of Jason and the Argonauts you can have the best ship and the best crew in the world but if you haven't got a golden fleece to searched for then you'd be lost. If you going to accomplish anything you have to dream big, think big, fail big. I feel the biggest challenge most people have is thinking big they think to small because they are afraid to fail. There is a high chance you will fail and fuck up, but so what! Really what the worst case - you have learned and grown and maybe for 5 seconds look silly. I told you when you learn to have no shame then you won't care because to me failure is being on your death bed with your loved ones around you – your hopes, all your ideas, dreams and ambitions, in a ghost form looking at you and dying with you because you cant give them to someone. Regrets will destroy you bit by bit just because you were to scared to let your inner self and everyone around you stop you failing.

"knowing you have failed to live up to your own standards is the ultimate pain knowing that you have fulfilled your highest vision is the ultimate pleasure"

Tony robbins :American life coach business owner

So I just wanted you to understand that rejection and failure are some of the toughest things, but part of the journey. The things you discover about yourself along the way are worth it to help discover what you can become. I know that I am going to fail a lot more in my life in all different aspect. What I'm really trying to get to is that you can fail to succeed in whatever you want to do and whatever goals you have, please just go for it in life! You will have people who want you not to, to stay the same not to push yourself, stay miserable and stay in the life that you are currently in; but I can guarantee you that all you'll pass is the nothing test, the test of being someone who wished they just tried. That to me is far more scary thing than failing on my arse and people laughing at me or not supporting my efforts or dreams.

Whatever age you are promise yourself be accountable, be someone that you can look at in the mirror and know you tried everything!

I'll tell you now as I started to write this book and move on to the next chapter of my life I am doing a lot for me and for my son Harry - because I have to succeed to give him the best life I can – so I have to go again ever time I think what are you doing Andy? I look in the mirror at myself I think people are counting on me, one day I know my son's going to ask me question in life and if you have kids or you want kids one day you need to be able to answer their questions. Be there for them show them that the most important thing they can do is to have the courage to face your fears and show that you did it even if you it took time and you failed you got back up and tried again to achieve your goals . Its being brave enough to do what you want and taking accountability for your actions and the things you want. You have to show other and prove people wrong because the day that child or person asks you those hard questions you need to have the answers to help start them on their journey. It's a bit like the Olympic Torch being past from one person to the next, what you do has an impact on your environment and those around you so be ready or start getting ready but most importantly be prepared to fail during the road to success and you will be able to show the next person the steps to becoming the best version of themselves.

The Safety Net

My dad always told me you should have a month's salary in my bank account just in case of a rainy day! That was good advice when I was 12 years old and a solid fundamental to start from. However, the world has changed since then and you have to adapt to this and also my own desire and knowing that I have dyslexia sacred the shit out me! I used to think how am I going earn good money if I cant even read ? Will I be able have a good life if I can't used a computer or write letters (I never needed to worry).

From early on I knew that I had to somehow learn about saving and putting money away just in case I lost my job or could find someone who would take me on. I know you're reading this now thinking "on top of all this you will be saying seriously stop Andy you shitting me we going to talk about money !!!" Yes we are - the thing everyone wants an everyone hates the metals or paper that makes men and women do almost anything as Bruce Forsyth would say if" the price is right" (kids check old Brucey out!).

Myself I am shit crap rubbish with maths!!! Hang on your be thinking you have done engineering you have to be good at maths! In some areas yes - I have learnt over the years tool-making which you have be spot on "measure twice cuts once" as they say but in other areas I've worked in knowing how to get something started and running again is far more important!. A lot of people with dyslexia I've spoken to struggle with understanding money. In fact I know most people struggle with it and just sit and panic and worry about how they are going to get that job or how they are going to make money for themselves and their families. Will they be able get enough salary for a house, car, a holiday or just to pay bills It can be unbelievably scaring when you are struggling to understand money. Just adding subtracting prices of stuff for years is hard I hated the feeling being in a shop and not understand if I had enough money to buy something or get a ticket for a train or pay a bill.

With dyslexia reading signs (see later in the book) and going places I would say 90% affect their lives and decision making on life and doing stuff day to day. I am going to tell you something that some of you may know but some of you may have no idea - but I think it will make a real different in your outlook and life goals but at the same time give you a chance to take that feeling of fear and how you going to cope with money and nail the relationship with money better. NOW super disclaimer I am no way a finical advisor I'm not telling you must do this or putting a gun to your head but just being honest with you if you are 16 years old or a parent with children with or even without maybe try this and give your children a chance (or yourself if you are the 16 year old) I have done this with my children and fingers cross it will give them some kind of freedom to do what they want and help them on the ladder of life.

This parts of the book is about steps of helping you get on that right financial track and try and support you on it till you get to the top of the ladder and look back down and think wow I actually got here I achieved it! To the "no you can't people" pull you pants down and shit on them or you can be the better person and carry on up learning and helping others.

We will all fail at some point with money - I have at different points in my life had nothing been hugely in my overdraft, had credit cards and even at some points been at the bookmarkers hoping that that win on the horse (Black Apache in the grand national will support me) but as my Grandad (a man I adore in every way) told me when he used to take me to the bookies in Battersea "don't bet what you cant afford to lose" priceless literally priceless advice the best tip ever!!!

The best advice I can give you is if you are having a baby or planning to have a family you need to future proof for them. I have set up stocks and share account for Harry so that his life will be less of a struggle... now your thinking shut up I have no idea about stocks I'm not pissing wolf or wall street, Jorden Belfort with braces on looking at graph!! But just listen if I can do it you can do it!

You've opened a bank account great, good start and you've got a job amazing you have already achieved more them most people! As a parent you want to the best start for your kids but no matter how old your child is (although the earlier you start the better) and your child diagnosed with dyslexia they will have a financial backup to help support them. If that are really struggling with their education but have a dream a standard savings account will give you maybe 0.25% or 0.5% or a introduction rate 1.5/2% great but will not help build a pot to support them or at the very least make their life a little easier. I have no right to tell you what to do with financial decisions...I'm certainly not a millionaire or massively well off if I was I be straight on a plane I would be sitting in Barbados on the beach with my missus well maybe not the beach (we both hate the beaches) ever since I was 9 years old going to Spain or Cyprus (I was very lucky I thank my mum and dad working 2 jobs each for this) getting sand in all places and sticking to you sunburn because I didn't listen to my mum to put cream on and walking up every bloody hill (there is always hill!!) in the sun because dad didn't want get a taxi with the sun burning on your back – begging not to have to walk. All you want is to have a cold shower. Sorry off the track a little there. I mean me and my missus drinking cocktails overlooking the beach with kids playing laughing at everyone who has to go to work on a Monday. Sadly I'm not there yet…to get on the road maybe is to set up account with Hargreaves Lansdown or any other trading company. Read up about it and make the best choice that fits you but for the children I opened an account and stick 4% of my wages in to it and every month its like a taxes in my head it automatic and I don't think about it and also every time I earn a little bit of extra money I automatic pay more with it it's called compounding interest.

I don't know everything I'm not money guru ask Martin Lewis for that or like I did start reading investment books like Ray Dailo now Ray is one of the most successful people in the world and guess what his is dyslexic! What interested me so much is that the way he goes about his investment I honestly believe and its proven that people who are dyslexic can see the bigger picture. What I feel makes me learn and so interested in the market is not the numbers not the company not the algorithms that these clever people develop with computer system but it's the relationship between things and the history or global markets and economy its the pictures and patterns for me. If you start learning this then you don't have to worry about millions of numbers. Again I'm not an expert I'm just telling you what I see and If you have dyslexia I believe you will see it as well.

So look below at three things I think you as a dyslexic can master or see which will hopefully help you created that safety net:

1: Cycles - so when I look at history of a country and its relationships with other countries you can see how I think a country will perform so for example the Roman empire in Italy built their commodities then exported to other countries in trading; this is called the bubble.

Then Rome was rich and invested in other countries infrastructure building roads. In trading terms this is called the top. Once Rome reached the peak of its powers…you guessed it just like a heavyweight boxers you will eventually lose a fight and everything you have built. In trading terms this is called the depression. After years the Roman market then stabilized in it position or in trading terms this is called normalization.

You can see this happen in every market history of the world Great Britain, Germany Greeks, Brazil, Russia, Japan and the USA. It may take 20 years or a 100 years but the same pattern will repeat again and again. I feel once you understand this you can see patterns in how a country start acting when listening to global news where this country is heading in the market.

2: Relationship and main assets – I'm not talking about if you make a great couple with the best looking bloke in school office or women with the best boobs - what I see and a lot of people with dyslexia can see easily in relationships things most people cant. For explain Ecuador in South America has one of the best coffee trades in the world but would it sell to its friends or someone they don't like? Its friends - so who are their friends (at the moment anyway!!) Brazil UK, Italy and Columbia. Who are they not so friendly with USA Mexico and Russia. So when Ecuador has something good to sale its going sell to its mates first right? So, if you want invest money into a company you want invest in the product and its mates not who it not so friendly with this is why history is so important when you are looking at the world markets which will help you to building money for yourself .

3: Look at the graphs and charts when you are looking to buy stocks or shares in a company, look how its perform over the years not what its currently doing. So many people who don't think like this lose so much because they are not you and their brains are not wired like yours. Look at the charts you don't need to see all the percentages or the big numbers look at the lines just like a football league team positioning .i.e. Season 1 finish 3rd season 2 finish 10th season 3 finish 14th season 4 finish 1st you can break it down to basics and see that this team is ok. You can then make the best choice for you if. The graphs are key to these three things.

I feel this is why I enjoy learning about the market and stop the usual barriers of being scary because of reports and big numbers dyslexics can see past this and enjoy learning about the world because once you can put the dots and line together and relationship of countries and history you start to love learning and it might help you and your family not worry about the future .

If possible try reading about Warren Buffet or Tony Robbins get their books take out of them what you can but always look at the charts the most simplest way I can explain this is this is picture of investment calendar attached.

Enter details of your investment

Enter the amount you currently have £ 0

Enter the amount you will invest each **month** £ 100

Calculate estimated returns based on the following ra
returns:

Low: 4 %
Medium: 7 %
High: 10 %

Results

After year	Low return value	Medium return value	High return value
5	6,630	7,159	7,744
10	14,725	17,308	20,484
15	24,609	31,696	41,447
20	36,677	52,093	75,937
25	51,413	81,007	132,683
30	69,405	121,997	226,049
35	91,373	180,105	379,664
40	118,196	262,481	632,408
45	150,947	379,259	1,048,250
50	190,936	544,807	1,732,439

Now for an example of saving!

So you are 16 years old and have a job or part time job somewhere and you get £400.00 a month £100.00 a week. You now set up this account up yes it will be so hard you might think at first its not worth doing but get in to the habit and it is easy! Its one weeks wage that £100 a month start hard but as you earn more money bonus' new job £100 will not be tough… lets do a little maths…for fuck sake Andy I hear you say!

Start age 16 pay £100.00 a month for 20 years you age will be 36 with compounding rates avenge at a year and after is

4 % = each year = £36,677

7% = each year £52,093

10% = each year £ 75,937

Well to me it's a no brainer it may not sound much to some but just by doing that you may just help yourself a little, give you or your kids a chance. That a house deposit or a car or university fees maybe! The big warning and as I've said before stock go up and down it is a gamble and you CAN loose. It can make 10% up one years and drop 15% the next year but over a period I believe and hope you will come out on top I really, really wish someone at 16 years old would of told me this. I just believe it's a better bet then put a £100 a month on the 2.45pm at ascot!?

"genius is one percent inspiration and ninety-nine percent is perspiration"

Thomas Edison inventor of the electric power generation,
mass communication sounds motion pictures

Chapter 5:
Gym Not Jim

"the mind is incredible once you've gained mastery over it channelling its powers positively for the purposes you can do anything I mean anything the secret is to make your mind work for you not against you this means constantly being positive constantly setting up challenges you can meet either today next week or next month I cant should be permanently stricken from your vocabulary especially the vocabulary of your thoughts you must see yourself always growing and improving"

Arnold Schwarzenegger 7x Mr Olympia

So now your going to say to me seriously Andy what the hell has lifting weights or exercise or whoever Jim is got to do with dyslexia? For me I believe this is one of the most important aspect which has not only change a lot in my life but help me build the foundation and fundamentals to achieve a better life style and outcome - and not just overcoming dyslexia but actually homing in on my gifts that I feel it comes with having it! Firstly as the chapter title goes JIM is not just a pun or something funny it's a dear friend of mine who taught me a life lesson that I will never forgot but more importantly help in my mindset as time has gone on.

Jim Powell was not only someone I worked with on the railway, and a friend but a brilliant man because of how he treated people and how he acted himself. What Jim taught me was that he didn't get a SHIT about what people thought about him or what he did. Jim didn't need permission from anyone, he did what made him happy! He would come in care free telling about what he been up to that weekend or plan that night. Or sometimes we would go off somewhere together and do stuff in and out of work! I didn't have that attribute or quality at the time, Jim push me out of my comfort zone. Sadly Jim passed away in 2015 and didn't get the change to do all the things that he always talk to me about what he was going to do when he retired.

He gave me something that was inside of me but needed to come out. Its in you too, you can feel it deep down when you at work, home, college or a job - you know that whatever you're doing your not happy doing. Or that time you didn't speak up when you knew the answers just in case you got it wrong and someone laughed at you. Once you realise this and execise it (see how I linked this it ha-ha) it then you as a person will blossom., just as I did.

I feel is one of the greatest individual things I have achieved in my life! Its also one of the best thing have taken into all areas of my life which has help me enhanced my ability with dyslexia. To get a complete understanding of what I mean lets start with 12 year old Andy - as I said before my body was changing and developing and girls stared coming on the scene!! Also I advanced in football as I started to get stronger I play up in age groups above me which would be tough to play against. At that time I loved Rocky films and ask my parents if I could have some weights for Christmas. Well Christmas day came and I did they got me these gold sand filled York weights with two barbell hands and a 15kg Olympic style bar so that was it! I watched Rocky 1, 2 or 3 (3's my favourite with Clubber Lang - Mr T - If you never seen it you must watch IT - bucket list job.

Anyway I set the weights up and work through the picture instruction that came with it and did as many reps as I could until that body part hurt (which later on helps) at the times I couldn't understand counting and the whole reps things I couldn't read or understand just yet, image a young me in the smallest room in the house with my bed and cupboard in between trying to do this with a movie cd of the rocky songs blaring out.

This was the start of my love for weight training then the art of bodybuilding. My dad joined a local hotel gym and stared taking me. My sister was friends with the owner/manager of the gym and I used to take my Dad's pass or he start chatting to the receptionist and I would sneak in behind him - we did this for two years until the bloke left and my dad stop going.

About this time I got to the stage where I had out grown that gym and had a desire to really learn and use better equipment. I did love going with my Dad and I discover and learnt how to do the basics I also learn how to not do things in the gym from other members. The gym is a great place for a young person to develop communication skills learning about other in a usual environment and gain confidence. I really feel it befitted me in later life and I would say is one of the biggest driving forces and help shaped the person I have become.

I will forever be grateful to a man I have always seen as a hero in my eyes who helped me progress as a man and a body builder (you can read more about him later) Ian Denman.

28th February 2016 at 18.00

At this time in my personal life was…lets just say a mess and my metal mind set was as bad as a beach in Normandy in 1944! It was also a month and bit until my greatest inspiration and sole purpose in life was born. I was 112 kg I have shown you a picture to prove it go on my Facebook page . I knew I had to make myself proud again for myself but also for my little soon to be in the world Harry. So on the above date and time I change my life for the better and rang Ian. I explain what was going on and happen and he came back with "right I get 100s of people asking me to train them and give them diets for competing and most fail" he gave me a plan for 12 weeks and told me to come back after the 12 week and if I completed it he would help me otherwise don't bother wasting his time!

That was it I wanted to prove to myself and to this man who in the pasted I had looked up to and wanted to be in most ways! I'm telling you from the beginning you have to make that commitment no matter what sets you on your course whatever your trigger may be (hopefully its this book) you have to stop the excuses of dyslexia holding you back and release the gift you have within. Just go for it whatever aspect of your life it is just start one brick at a time, or for me one curl, one bench press or one squat at a time. Once I started all my heart aging, stress started to melt away. In that space and time for one or two hours it all stopped. Then my decision making, ideas and life style choices began to improve. My self development and awareness was growing, the same as my muscle were developing. As this process happened I want you to understand how exercising for just 30 minutes a day 3-5 times a week will transform you brains development which in turn will help you overcome and improve every aspect on your life.

One of my top tips if you have a computer or an I-phone or I-pad download or look up Ted talks and watch a woman called Wendy Suzuki. Wendy discover that 30 minutes exercise a can protect you from illness, moods swings and help with behavioural issue. It will also improve brain functions such as memory and brain cognitive skills helping to develop the whole prefrontal cortex and temporal lobe. She has discovered that your brain function can be improved by up to 50% just by exercising for 30min a day. The other area it is shown to improved is the hippocampus this is so important to people with dyslexia as this is the area of the brain most affected by dyslexia. So you can see just how important this can be toward your brain development.

Currently in Scotland a company called Step (which I would love to see brought down to England) is currently using exercise before classes in school to help children with dyslexia and other disability like ADHD. Below shows the improvements of children's who are using this program of exercise before class and you can see the results tables which truly show how this has improved their performance in class.

Chapter 5: Gym Not Jim

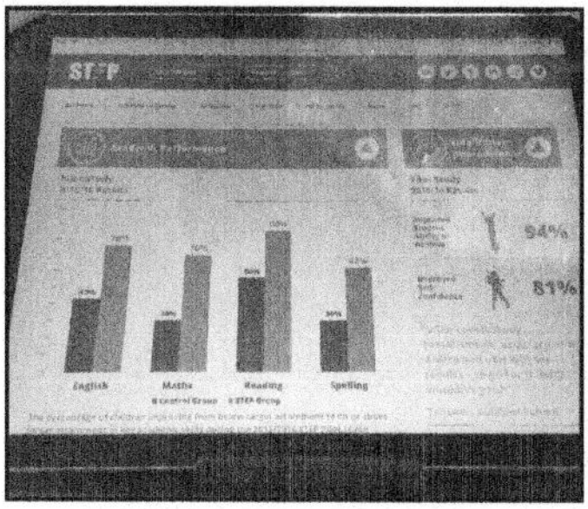

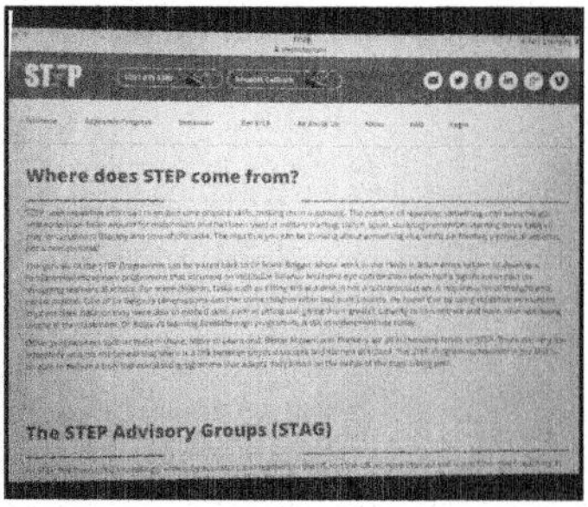

As well as exercise I changed by diet from my own personal experiences - this is not the answer for everyone and I'm not say to try this, but for me it worked. I went and researched and changed to a diet called Keto, this is a low-carb, high fats diet. There has been a lot of research that has shown marked improvements in heath and functionality for people who have diabetes, cancer, epilepsy, Alzheimer and behavioural issues. For me when I went into a state called ketosis (which you will go into after a few weeks you feel like your getting a cold but you don't) I found that my thinking, decision making and most importantly for me my grammar and reading skill dramatically improved! I found that what I explain later in the tips section (see chapter 8) that I didn't need aids to help me read it was so much clearer in my mind and I went from reading maybe 4/6 pages in a day to 20/30 pages a day! This wont be for everyone but I honestly think that people with dyslexia that Ketogenic diets can help open the pathways and the help in the brains process of building myelin. What myelin do you mean the women who was in Liberty X the band and now does Marks and Spencer adverts - no I mean MYELIN this is a sheath that goes round your brain pathways. Just as I said in chapter 3 about paths myelin is like the cover around electrical wires.The bigger the myelin the sheath the quicker the messages can be sent and guess what myelin can build just like your muscle so repetition, repetition and more repetition it will really help build the myelin which in turn will help your brain and you develop. If you haven't heard of the 10,000 hours rule then look up and read a book called bounce by Matthew Syed who won the commonwealth table tennis championships and resented great Britain in two Olympic games.

Right little off tack as I'm sitting in a dark room working and writing this bit at 3.25 am!!

On the 1st June - 12 weeks later - I went back to Ian having followed his training plan and diet. I had proven I was committed and I started the next step from there every week twice a week including Saturday morning after having done the night feeds with Harry I would go down the gym in Brighton East Sussex with Ian and his lovely wife Lorraine and we would train hard, my body would be in pieces and it would be telling me to stop give up! Each week that pasted my mind became more resistant it helped me push all my stress and worries away and I was becoming me again. As I said at the beginning the most important thing for you the reader at whatever age or how you feel that you should never worry about what people say or think about you.

Chapter 5: Gym Not Jim

I had so many people say you can't go on stage – you're not good enough or look at me funny when talking about competing. Actually the same as have you probably always had when someone talks to you or discuss something and you have the confidence to tell them you have dyslexia you suddenly get a different look or they would start to look at you funny or stop talking! Nowadays I am interested to watch people's reactions when I tell them because they don't know I am as it's not printed on my head or I don't represent their idea of what it is. So next time it comes up do me a favour and tell someone and see what there do - it's a good judge in business I find that people who are not bother or comment on how well you cope or are surprised at how you deal with it are people you want in your life.

As the months past and the weights went up the reps built up and the diet got tougher my body transformed and at the time I focused on making my son proud when ever it got too much. As the day of the competition came standing in a spay booth the other competitors came in and I felt tiny compared to them. At one point I was in a toilet block away from it all and my sister Karen was with me I was pumping my body with resistance bands before getting called and I look in the mirror and through what the fuck are you doing Andy my size, my proportion and symmetry was not as good as most in my class. Then my sister pulled out a bottle of white wine and said drink some of this! It's a great tip I was told to use the night before and on the day to help with dehydrate the skin help the muscle development show more – it really works by the way! I hammered it down and my sister said something that I never forget. Karen "you have inspired me little bruv the amount of people who couldn't do this I'm proud of you" I looked back in that mirror and started laughing with her thinking this is mad but bollock lets have a laugh the call came over the speaker to get backstage. As I arrived everyone I was against was there and hitting the weights one of the other lads came up to be and said can you hold this band I want to do my back rows so I did and was thinking having no idea what to do next so I just copied him. We got chatting and he was a good bloke he was smaller then me but had a really good condition body as we spoke I relaxed I realised (good lesson here) everyone is feeling the same as you! I think at that time sport physiology plays a part but deep down everyone is worrying and its just how you cope and deal with it make the impact. Anyway we lined up backstage next to me this chap called Tom Colemen who I believe will be Mr Olympia one day and at that time the current British Champion!! Crap! Then the long months training kicked it I thought fuck it I'll do it for me and Harry and who cares what others say - that people is the best feeling in the world to not worry about other people, fear is one of the biggest thing as a human but there is nothing to fear in life, so I say hello Tom my name Andy and this is my first ever show Tom said "really! Fair play mate I remember my first show" that was it we talk for a bit and then the announcer started calling the line-up out.

Tom is a really top bloke and even though he was about go on stage he took time to support and help me before going on. Next the announcer calls number "17 ANDY WEBB" I took a massive breath and walked out to the bright lights I went out and performed to the best of my ability and loved every minute of it!

The best way I can explain being on stage is that for a couple minutes when you are doing your own individual posing routine everyone's looking at you and maybe wishing or wants to be like you. You get to control the way you want to be seen and to be you completely for that short time. You look like you may never look again. People may laugh at you but deep down you had the balls to get up there! When I got off stage I found my Mum and Dad and my sister Karen (who loved coming back stage and helping drink white wine before the show and is something special we shared - that chat in a toilets in the building never forget sis). Ian and Lorraine were also there to support me. I felt amazing!! I came seventh but I felt like I had won, I was overwhelm by how may people came to congratulate me and said they loved my routine.

To end this chapter like the end of a Rocky films – if I can change and do it then you can too. Do whatever you want to and achieve something greater than you believe is possible. I'm certainly not saying go into bodybuilding but what I'm saying is that once you find that trigger and take that first step and go for it then you become that person everyone is looking at wishing it was them. Don't let anything including dyslexia hold you back. I tell you that visualising your goals and going after it will change your life forever and you may just have fun in the process. I couldn't wait to get back to the gym and because every rep felt like I as taking me one step closer to achieving something, realising my dreams and bettering myself in ways I thought I could never ever do. I have now found it hard to understand how you can't do 30/45min in a day excised to improve yourself both in mind and body.

Lets break it down you have 24 hours in a day – lets say 6 hours at most sleeping or in bed, if you can get more great but if you have kids 6 hours is a miracle! So this leave you 18 hours so average Joe - works 10 hours (lets hope you work less but giving an average) so that leave us 8 hours, now lets say you travel 2 hours a day including picking up and dropping off kids - so now your left with 6 hours - so you cook dinner watch TV sort the kids out that leaves you 2 hours left…so now just do 30-45min of physical exercise which will improve your mental state and well being. You are still lefts 1 hour and 15min (minimum) so plan get organised there is no excuse to not try your best at something you enjoy or love to do.

Chapter 5: Gym Not Jim

Like the chapter before this is not a set of must do rules its just ideas and a guide to help you to think about things and how to potentially improve your life. It maybe none of the interests you at all and that's fine. These are technics that I use and helped me. I feel that to get you where you may want to go and spend how ever long you been on this planet that in order to move forward and improve you need to stop the excuses that you cant because of dyslexia or life experiences. You can do whatever you like (within realms of reality) in this life.

If you are interested in improvement and want an idea of what I did to improve my physical and mental health below is the diet that Ian put me on to start my fitness journey (before I moved on to Keto) It's a great starter diet for all fitness needs and will help kick start your training whether you just want to get fitter or have a specific need for cardiovascular endurance or for a specific sport then you need to look at what you eat diet is key.

Here is an example of diet for you to follow. You can adjust it to your taste and add some light sauces or flavourings if you wish.

Can't stress enough they Also drink minimum 3 litres water per day.

- on waking........ Multi vits
- **7am** 80 oats with 1 x banana with water40g whey protein
- **10am** 150g chicken, 30g (dry weight) rice or 120g sweet potato mixed with
  1 x T spoon olive oil, black pepper 50g broccili
- **1pm** 1 x tins tuna mashed with 200g sweet potato, 50g veg 1 x t sp olive oil
- **4pm** 100g chicken or white fish with 150g white jacket potato1 x small banana
- **6.30pm** (Post workout) 50g whey protein maltadextrose to give you 60gcarbs
  5g creatine 10g glutamine 1000mg Vit C
- **8.30pm** 250g chicken, steak, fish with 200g mixed veg
- **10.30pm** 50g whey protein or 150g chicken.
  1000mg vit C 25mg zinc or ZMA minimum 3 litres water per day,

You might be thinking what do you know about it? Well not wanting to be smug but whilst writing this chapter I decided I wanted to carry on and do what I love, so whilst writing this I decided to created my company Destiny Performance and now I have obtained my Level 3 diploma in fitness, instructing and personal training and boot camp training I am a Level 4 Strength and Condition Coach and I currently have around 30 clients on packages that are changing people lives. This is what I love doing so much now I will talk more about this soon but if ever you want to speak to me or take it up I will at the end of this book leave my company details guess what I yes I will actually get back to you I have done it in the past when I have read a book and want to know something or get and answer to something or just say how much you enjoy it and you get nothing from them at all!!

I've put on the following page just a small training plan 5 session start off with 30min cardio a day like I said before and then 4-5 session a week with the muscle development plan and a picture of my final week before going on stage a picture of the keto pyramid.

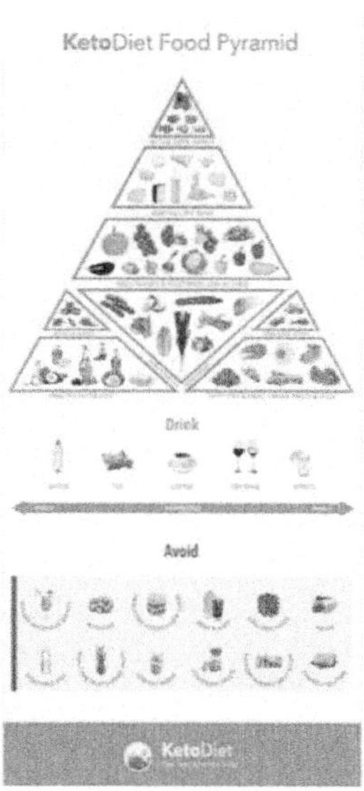

ANDY WEBB LAST WEEK

	WATER	VIT C	TRAINING
SUNDAY	3L	3G	CHEST TRICEPS
MONDAY	3.5L	3G	BACK BICEPS
TUESDAY	4L	4G	SHOULDERS
WEDS	4.5L	4G	ARMS
THURSDAY	5L	5G	WHOLE BODY (NO LEGS) 1 X EXERCISE 5 X SETS OF 15
FRIDAY	6L	6G	REST

Food as normal, on day of show just eat as hungry, tke some rice cakes and honey or nutella spread so you can have a bit of carbs hour before stage if you want
Stop drinking water &pm friday nigh keep taking 1g Vit C every 2 hours up to stage, day of show just sip water
Smash cardio up till thursday hen complete rest

keep In touch ian

This is an example of diet I started to follow. If you fancy this You can adjust it to your taste and add some light sauces or flavourings if you wish . Cant stress enough the Also drink minimum 3 litres water per day.

on waking........ Multi vits

7am 80g oats with 1 x banana with water

40g whey protein

10am 150g chicken, 30g (dry weight) rice or 120g sweet potato mixed with

1 x T spoon olive oil, black pepper 50g broccili

1pm 1 x tins tuna mashed with 200g sweet potato, 50g veg 1 x t sp olive oil

4pm 100g chicken or white fish with 150g white jacket potato

1 x small banana

6.30pm (Post workout) 50g whey protein maltadextrose to give you 60gcarbs

5g creatine 10g glutamine 1000mg Vit C

8.30pm 250g chicken, steak, fish with 200g mixed veg

10.30pm 50g whey protein or 150g chicken.

1000mg vit C 25mg zinc or ZMA

minimum 3 litres water per day,

Chapter 5: Gym Not Jim

Workout 1 Shoulders:

1. Press behind neck barbell 5set 15-12-10-8-15 reps
2. Dumb bell side raises 4x12 reps
3. Barbell up rights rows 3x12 reps
4. Seated dumbbell shoulder press 3x12 reps
5. Barbell shrugs 4x15 reps

Workout 2 Back:

1. Wide grips chins 4x12 reps
2. Barbell bent over rows 3x12 reps
3. Seated cables row 3x12 reps
4. Dumbbell pullovers 3x12 reps
5. Lat pulldowns 3x10 reps

Workout 3 Legs/Calves

1. Squats 5x 12-10-8-6-12 reps
2. Leg extensions 4x12 reps
3. Stiff leg dead lift 3x15 reps
4. Leg press 5x 15-12-10-8-6 reps

Workout 4 Chest

1. Flat bench press 5x set 12-10-8-6-15 reps
2. Flat bench dumbbell flies 4x10 reps
3. Incline dumbbell press 4x10 reps
4. Cable crossovers3 x12 reps
5. Peck decks 3x10 reps

Workout 5 Arms

1. Triceps pushdown 4x12 reps
2. Incline tricep press 4x10 reps
3. Narrow grip bench press 3x12 reps
4. Standing barbell curls 4x10 reps
5. Seated dumbbell 4x12 reps
6. Cable preacher 3x10 reps

"Imagination is more important then knowledge. Knowledge is limited imagination encircles the world"

Mr Albert Einstein

Chapter 6:
M.I.N.D Strengths & Set

OK so this is chapter is not some mind control power Voodoo stuff what I'm going to show is a anagram that explains the four areas that people with dyslexia tend to have as characteristics. Things that we do better then anyone else in the world - how cool does that sound I feel like some super hero when writing/ reading this - just as in chapter 3 we will delve into to the in depths of each of these amazing traits. I hope I can help you better understand why being dyslexic is a gift because in part of these skills. Whilst everyone is different and their skills can vary these talents or gifts as I would call them have been proven in many studies to be common in people with dyslexia. We have the ability to perceive relationship between things like similarities, groupings minute differences, far reaching implications, gaps and imbalances. Something I feel is very strong is the three dimensional spatial reasoning and mechanical ability. To perceive and manipulate subtle patterns in complex and constantly shifting systems and data. The ability to remember and understand abstract information.

Material reasoning

We can paint a picture in our mind like a blueprint a 3D image of a drawings of a house. Someone who is dyslexic can turn a 2d picture or object and transform this in our heads. We can imagine the route in full pictures if you give us directions, we can literally walk it in our heads as if it was already built this is why we are so good at map reading and locational skills. We have the ability to interconnect skills that make us into very creative people. I believe that dyslexics are very late bloomers and we shouldn't be judged by standard classroom tasks or tests. I believe that a child with dyslexia should be given Lego or creative toys to help them discover and develop their creative side which will help the teachers to find that child's talent through what seem like play but involves creativity in a non stressful way in school and help develop it instead of doing maths test, paper exams other languages (a bit later in the book I explain my own ideas of what the school system should or maybe could do in the future) as I hope by doing this we can help the next engineers, scientists and inventors break through to new life design that may to help us all. When football scouting we look at how a child are skilled and how best to advance that skill.

- Entrepreneurship we can visualise ideas, create a company or a plan of action before it is real or on paper.
- Engineering we can see and breakdown parts like myself I see things like a Hayes manuals at times

- Architecture (like above) seeing that building in our mind - creating that piece of reality for others that buildings already built and the surrounding environments
- Arts creating that piece of magic or off the cuff writing acting story telling performing that part as if they were there in the moment of time in history
- Sport seeing that pass or point how to paint the picture or move before it happens to win the point or pass the player or check mate the other team patterns shapes, tactics reading of the game .

Interconnected reasoning

We as dyslexics have a fantastic way of looking a pieces of information that don't make sense or relationship between them - we can connect all these bit together and bring new ideas in to place for example:

- There are people in a room chatting in a group - a woman says "I cant get home I haven't got my purse on me or my phone to ring a taxi" and then a women in the group say; she hasn't got any money but she has a car and doesn't know if she will be able in fill it up this week after a few trips. As a dyslexic - you can pick this picture very quickly! The light goes off you can help both people in a second, which is what happened with the founder of Uber and now a multimillionaire now.

- Back in 1999 a English phycologists John Everatt carry out two tests for dyslexia. He tested people with and without out dyslexia and found that the cognitive test which involved patterns and relationships. People with dyslexia out performed those without and scored on average 30% better than people without dyslexia. I did a similar test myself with the relationship of words and how they are connected - in the test I remember it asking me what do you think about the words blue and grey? Most people would say they are colours. No not me I said they were the colour of the uniforms of the army in the American civil war! Another question was what you think of the words Benson and Hedges and Marlborough? Most people word say cigarettes. My answer was the two sponsor for Formula 1 cars teams Jorden and McLaren! After the test they said to me that I scored in the top 3% in interconnected reasoning it's the first time ever I been in the top 3 percent in life woohoo!

Narrative reasoning :

Is the gift of being able to construct a connected a series of scenes in the mind from fragments of past personal experience to help develop and explain present simulation potential, future or imaginary scenarios and understand or test important concepts. For example: Boy A asks his mum and dad for a bike because he would like one and all the other kids have a bike and he wants to ride with them. Boy B -asks his mum and dad if you could buy me a bike you wouldn't have to take me to football training on a Saturday and you can stay in bed or relax with your coffee in the morning and not rush. SEE what I mean building a compelling story!

This an area where writers like Steven Spielberg or comedian Eddie Izzard find that purpose or gift can you image no star wars, ET, Jurassic park or Eddie's humorous story telling.

Dynamic reasoning

As dyslexics an ability to see past events which can allow us to predict future out comes. Now before you laugh and think he's lost the plot! I don't mean we can see what this weekend football results will be otherwise I would not be writing this book and having a cry because its one am in the morning and my brain can't spell a word. What I mean is we see beyond the picture being painted for example if you are being taught about erosion in school in geography i.e. water falls from the sky through the mountains into a river causing erosion. Someone without dyslexia would stop there. People with dyslexia would with out being taught predict what would happen next and consider all other environmental consequences of the that initial rain drop. Instead of turning the next chapter/topic to learn about plates (not the dinner style ones) what happen if more rain came the river built up into a lake then the lake fills up turn into a ocean and so on and so on.

You my have read this and are thinking I don't have any of these traits what are you talking about BUT you do its in you just like I said in previously it takes time to develop your brain like a muscle – it can take years and years to unlock your potential but once you do you will see these four aspect come into your life and your mind will show you this.

Working on your strength, not your weaknesses.

I believe that and you might not agree with me, but there are things in life you're not good at simple as that. There are certainly things that you're never going to be. You could be 10% good at science or maths. I'm not great at maths at all and I went on to do engineering, don't know what happened there! I'm joking now.

What I really fundamentally believe is as a person you should go and give something 100% if you are brilliant at it. You should of cause always try other things and learn new skills, but if you're 20% good at maths and then you only get up to 40%, what is the point? If you're 80% good at a certain skill, you can be 100% at it and be the best in this field then why not give everything in that area?

Every person in this world has a gift. You are talented at something. I don't know what your talent is, but you all have something, you all have a gift that makes a huge difference. For me personally to sit there and spend hours and hours and hours and hours on repetition, which is what I want you to do in some aspects, but to do it on something that you're only going to be all right at, today's society doesn't work like that. Our fundamental education system is wrong. And for you to sit there and spend hours on something you could actually be good at would make a huge difference.

Today if you want to find out the answer to an equation, you go on your phone. If you want to know about businesses or mortgages, you can find it out on the internet. You watch YouTube videos to learn how to do things. You want to fix a pipe, obviously you get a plumber in if you can afford it or you know one, but if not, you're going to do or at least try to do it yourself. You don't have to be the best at everything and that is the big thing that I want you read in this book to understand is that you don't have to anymore. The most famous, most successful people in the world are brilliant at one or two things. They're not brilliant at everything. They have other people for the things they are not good at they outsource and that is a huge thing I want to get across to you when you're doing stuff, is outsourcing makes a huge difference – it certainly does for me. I remember when I was younger and I purchased my first house, I wanted to do everything because I'm a man, I want to try and learn to do stuff, but I wasn't the best at everything. So I would spend hours trying to do it myself (I thought that's what I was supposed to do) whereas if I had paid (not always possible) an expert to do it, it would have been done in half the time. Nowadays I'd rather work 10- 12 hours somewhere else and work really hard, but then have enough money to pay someone else to do it. For example a cleaner, you know, I'd get a cleaner in to clean the house, which then saves me 2 or 3 hours, but if I'm paying that cleaner say £20.00, and say I earn £50.00 an hour, you work the maths out I've still got money left over and it makes a huge difference, plus I hate cleaning!

Again, with outsourcing, I have one of my best mates Dan who's part of my business, who's going to make my business more successful. He is brilliant at social media and with content ideas. I have ideas, but he puts them on there with his spin. I'm not going to spend hours trying to do this kind of thing as its not my strong point. Why would I stress myself out? I've got the imagination, I've got the plan in my head, I got an idea of what I want to project, but I can't do it. And it's frustrating. I spent years of doing that, Dan has a skill so he does it. It works.

I remember putting applications in for the fire service or other jobs and I would get stressed and take it out on other people because I couldn't do the application and I'd get them to help me, but they wouldn't understand what I wanted to put on the page from those experiences I've learned over time that if you've got an idea and if you can get someone who's an expert in it, get them to do it. Trust me. You will feel happier, gives you the ambition then to work harder to pay for that person, but at the same time, the weight and the balance, you got more free time to do other stuff that you're good at.

What I'm trying to say is work on your strengths, the things you're not good at, let someone else do. Trust me and it'll make your life so much better. 'exactly the same as I'm doing now I started by typing this book and it was hard then I thought about dictating so someone else could do the hard stuff for me, I've "written" a lot of this on a recorder as I got a company called Speechpad who then they transcribed the book, it's brilliant. If when I had started the book I had know about this program, it might have made the book quicker to do.

The biggest thing is that I've learned to outsource, I've got people to do stuff for me that I can't do myself. And I've massively learned as well that you have the old saying, "Jack of all trades, master of fuck all" that is so true. I'd rather be the master of one thing and give everyone else the opportunity to do everything else for me and be the Jack of traders.

We're taught as children to stand in line, do what everyone else does. We're told to get good grades at school, follow the crowd. Do what everyone else is doing. Go and get a job, get a safe pension, try and save ourselves not to run out of money before we end in retirement. If we do anything outside of this, then we are looked at as funny or weird. Break free from this.

Who's in your inner circle?

With whom you surround yourself is who you will become. I believe there are people who are battery chargers and people that are battery drainers. Now, obviously quite ironically with me, people know me on the railway. I used to install and build batteries when working at Network Rail. And this kind of concept came to me when I sat and I thought the people you surround yourself change your mood instantly. If you're with negative people, you become negative, you see the world in a different light. If you're with positive people, you have a positive experience. I think that's why I love football so much the coaches and people, you're surrounded in an environment of people with the same ideals as you. If you have a real passion or you've got an idea what you want to do, or you're surrounded with people that go it influences you and how you act.

When you are dyslexic, you hear a lot of "you can't do this, because you're dyslexic, you can't do that, because you're dyslexic, you've got to do this." Trust me it doesn't work like that.

I really think the more time that you surround yourself with positive people the better you become. If you want to be an entrepreneur, you start your own company, socialize with other entrepreneurs. If you want to be physically fitter and you want to get in better shape, you hang around with people in better shape. That is what you do. Surround yourself in the environment that you want to excel in.

This is the same for parents you want them to do their best, so you surround them with people that are positive for them, surround them with people going to help them achieve what they want to be, whatever it is. If you've got a young kid that says, "Do you know what? I want to ride motorbikes for a living. I love being on a motorbike," you would surround him or her with people that build motorbikes, surround him with people enjoy motorbike that are experts in that field. Help that child fully engage and encourage their dreams. Whatever they want to do, start helping them, surround them with people they are going to look as role models, look up to, help them, guide them, give them the path and structure they need.

All the things that I've wanted to do in my life. I've gone and got a mentor. I've found someone who I looked up to. I'd think right, if this is what I'm going to achieve, what is the blueprint for me? How am I going to get there? Because on my own, I may not achieve the level I need to achieve. This is something that's massively important.

You need help, a bit like outsourcing. Every aspect of my life I have someone that helps me in each section. Your story, your emotions, your faults, and your story are your life, it is who we are at the moment, and we protect these three things in everything we do. I might inspire you one day, two days after you read this book and then you drift back into your old story, your old habits, your old routines, your old chimp on your shoulder. You need an anchor in your life. An awareness. Hopefully that's me. You need something that's going to give you the tools to make that shift, to change that story you've been living with, to change your mental state, to develop the habits, the and the tactics to help you achieve wherever you want to be in life. So hopefully I've given you the confidence to get you to that next level.

Helping your finances in all areas of your life I just hope that what I am giving to you that you start change that story and don't hold back anymore of who you are. Believe in yourself, start finding the niche that you are good at and good things will follow.

There are so many people out there that feel that because they are dyslexic, I am limited, that they can never achieve their dreams or goals. I think dyslexia taught me to be able to communicate really simply and be really straight forward with different people. I believe that when I'm in groups that it gives me the confidence to be able to adapt to my environment. As Micky Flanagan says I'm a "social Shameleon" (said in cockney accent). I feel like I can put myself in any situation and adapt to it. And I think that's a skill for me from years of being able to talk to people because obviously I couldn't write it down. I think you've got to start making events that have happened to you help you to change. For example, the relationship with Harry's mum ended and because of this I changed my life for the better because Now I'm a better dad then I think I would have been because I had to evolve and learn from it. I sit here and I feel like, I've got in to the best shape of my life mentally and physically, and I believe that you've got to go through hardship to enable you to change and empower your own story.

Implement this tip quickly and you will see and feel the dramatically positive affects to your life in such a short period of time. This is the whole reason I've written this book to hopefully help people. So, keep pushing on, keep sticking with it, we've come this far, so don't stop now. As we continue on this journey through my book, I want you to start thinking about these new habits, processes and exercise, which is keeping the eye on the prize and change your behaviours now to make a massive difference in your life.

Four C's of confidence.

Now, let's look back at your life so far and the lack of confidence you've got because of your dyslexia. Have you ever been in position where you wanted to ask a girl out for dinner or talk to that boy when you were out? OR gone for coffee and you've not said a word and you've let that person slip away? Have you had the opportunity to tackle a tough project, build your own business, take action, but you've decided you're not to because you don't have the confidence to tackle it or someone around you has put doubts in your head? Have you ever refused to walk into a gym because you feel you're too out of shape and people are going to laugh at you? There are so many people who lack the confidence to do what makes them happy. This is what I want you to try and help you over come help you building your confidence.

This next section shows you how to start realizing the areas that you need to work on.

This is what I mean by the four C's.

Courage

Confidence

Commitment; and

Capabilities.

Below are the basic meanings, you can rip this page out keep it with you and start practicing theses four C's. As I've been saying throughout this book when you finish this I hope you wont be the same person with dyslexia I need you to start believing in yourself and people without dyslexia you can start becoming a role model a leader to others. Sometimes people will never achieved anything without someone else taking the first step - putting there hand out and saying I will show you, I will help you, I will support you support your ideas. Sir Roger Gilbert Bannister was the man who broke the 4min mile when no-one believed it could ever be done!

Courage :

- **Feeling fear yet I choose to act:** I used to be intimidated by people more successful then me. I used to think that because they had a better education then me they would know more than me. I used to think my company wouldn't last or grow because people had been doing it longer then me. Courage is to be judged more by someone you love then fear its self stops and you cease to fear what others think. You should only fear not showing the ones you love the whole you.

Follow your dreams do whatever you want to do just be brave as I've said what the worse that can happen

Persevering in face of adversity: you are going to fail your going to lose you are going to want to quit but every time you get up and start again its doesn't hurt as much if you go down again just keep trying – maybe look back at this book and at your progression

Stand up for what your believe in: your going to have people not liking or agreeing in or believing in what you want to achieve but think about what is important to you and why your doing it and push forward.

Expanding your world do something that's not familiar: if you do the same things week in week out and never come out of your comfort zone you will never develop do something new or learn something new whenever you can it will help expand your knowledge and give you more courage to go out an achieve your dreams.

Facing adversity with faith and dignity: life will throw you some real challenges and you have a choose but if you believe that in time life will improved and you are the one that will make the difference to your happiness. You will learn to walk tall and know you did you very best in whatever situation you find yourself in. People always remember the person that acted with class and dignity

Commitment

- **Conscientious** try do the best at what you do always give your all to the task you need to achieve your goal. Think about your game plan and how you will approach things before starting out.

- **Work hard** I mean when the opportunity arises work the hardest at whatever it is. Put it all on the line at least what ever your outcome you done everything you could

- **Focus:** now funnily enough it's hard to focus isn't it - but plan your time use it wisely and you will make a success of your life

- **Keep a promise** never let a person down if you promise you going to do it you must take ownership and accountability for your action and you will see your results

- **Set a targets** one year five years doesn't matter set that goal and design how your going to get there do whatever it takes.

Capabilities

To reach your full potential you must

- Exercise regularly
- Think about your body language towards others
- Achieve a task a day
- Learning something new make you better at your job and in life
- Eat correctly
- Setting yourself deadline and stick to them
- Sleep – get as much as you need some need 3 hours others 7 hours,
- Sleep routine before bed no TV, phone an hour before sleep.
- Make lists of ideas of task or goals you would like to achieve over a year and put away and go back every 6 months to see what you have achieved and what you need to push harder for.
- Take responsibility for you actions
- Accept what you cant control i.e. cant control weather and other people
- Embrace what you can control i.e. how you treat people

Confidence

Have the confidence in your abilities, skills and most importantly yourself

- Start talking to different people learn about them to build knowledge
- Watch people body language toward you and others to understand others needs
- Argue your corner never let anyone tell you are wrong if you honestly feel you are right try to help them understand your point of view whilst respecting their point of view – not an easy thing!
- Ask question check you fully understand before moving on to the next question or action.
- Wear clothes that make you feel good if you feel good you act good if you act good you become good and that's what you are trying to get to.

"every great dream begins with a dreamer"

Harriet Tubman: American activist nickname the conductors for saving hundreds of slaves to freedom in underground railroads

Chapter 7:
Habits Tatctics and Skills

Throughout this book I've given what I hope are tips or I guess lesson I believe helped me and will help you make the little shifts, the tiny little habits to progress my personal journey to be more successful. I hope they will make a impact in your life too.

I want to help you replace your old habits for these new more positive ones.

Before you try some of the things I've suggest below I want you to ask yourself is "What is your WHY?" you had a why for picking the book up! I look at it like this;.

Why did I write this book? Answer as above for me to help someone and to achieve something that is greater than me. I also did it for my son.

Then I asked my self "Why I want make a different to people, particularly to those most close to me" Bang my trigger! I wanted to created a legacy for my family for Harry and Issy and my Wife to be proud of me. I wanted the kids to know they have the choices and options that I never did as a kid.

I want the kids to be able choose where they want to go in life and have the ability to do it and become the best and happiest versions of themselves. To not have to worry about money but to also understand it use it carefully. I want to help them become whatever they want to be.

So trust me when you start asking this question "why" think hard about what is your why is. What was your trigger for buying this book? Once you do this you be able to try the below and become the best version of yourself. Its so easy to just read and do it then put the book down and let the habits the other chimp inside of you from (chimp paradox Prof Steve Peters) the little you on your shoulder making choices for you making you not believe in yourself or convince you to stop - don't write that application out to push on change your life. Do you know why I feel so strong about this because -

I know what its like to cry in your room

I know what is like to fail

I know what its like to panic and get hot face

I know what its like to feel stupid or make up a lie get you out of reading or paying for something or meet people to do stuff

I know so I want the habits and skill below to mean some thing to you. I want in two years time after doing theses things for you to email me, or text me or meet me and say thanks for helping me (or say andy you're a dickhead wasted my time reading your book got nothing from it-I hope not but cant please everyone) deep down I know if you would get one little shift in your life it would make a difference. I don't want you to mimic my life or try to be Orlando Bloom, Steve Jobs, Holly Willoughby I just want you to look back and not recognise that person anymore and be the best version of you.

I want dyslexia not to be thought of as a learning disorder or disability. I hope it will one day be reclassified and the concept that it's just a different learning style with people with specific gifts and talents. I want to change the perspective that dyslexia is some kind of horrible disease that make us less some how. If we change our thinking and the way we educated employ and teach individuals with dyslexia and don't think of people as damaged. Investing in their abilities and their futures and giving them the confidence to push forward would be life changing for dyslexics. Now, one of the first things I want you to try is this:

My wife Nadine inspired me when it came to this and ever since I have been doing this it has help me be honest with myself and with others. I call it – The Morgen Freeman conversation. I'm not religions I had never believed in it what so ever before. Whilst I don't believe I always hoped if it was true I would go upstairs or whatever there may be after. I had no real knowledge of religion. However, what I'm trying to say is Morgan Freeman is the closest thing to a god like figure that I know and his voice is incredible! Anyway my wife as taught me a bit about Lucifer, fallen angels, feet in the sand and Kane and Able. I've even been to church - I can't believe I didn't burn up!! I actually went after I said I would never go. We were in Rome and we when to a service on the Sunday in this amazing church (which I found out was in a Tom Hanks film Angels and Demon) I was sitting there she was listen to the priest and I was looking around and she went up in a line to take the bread and drink the wine. At this time I had some real struggles going on in my life and I found myself at peace in this place. To be clear I wasn't at peace with god or Jesus but it was nice to stop and think about life then my grandad came into my thoughts and I listened to his voice as I have done a lot before this as my Grandad was so important to me. He used to call me boy and we would walk down to the corner shop in Lavender Hill and he would just talk to me in his way, he was a tall good looking man with movie star good looks and a deep voice and always dressed smart. I always remember people always waving and crossing the street to greet him. Saying "Franky" or respectfully "Good Morning Mr Webb" as we walked he would hold my hand as say things to me like "Boy always take care of your women or conduct you self right, dress smart, or if someone hits you hit them back". I thought I wasn't really listening as I was thinking what sweets and gun is Grandad going get me but it stuck and I've always try to live by his guidance. I try to be honest.

This is what I'm getting to - my pearl of wisdom - Pick that person who you can not lie to, that one person who you respect or means a lot to you dead or alive but just have to tell the truth. Then you know what that person is going to say to you like my grandad does to me is "*why are you not living up to your best Boy*! I guided you into this world and I've been to war for you so what are you doing with your life?" What's going be your answer? I could never lie to him and you have to answer back what the excuse there isn't a excuse the damaged belief in myself I have had from what people have said to me and from the experiences I have had. I spoke back to my grandad and from that day I've been more honest with myself then ever and anytime that a old shitty experience, or words that hurt me or a rejection I experienced I think about what he would say or advise and I move forward regardless and never use the excuse "I cant because" (I know how to spell this word - big elephant can always upset small elephant - never forgot that one spelling lesson!) there is no "because" As Apollo Creed says in Rocky III "There is no tomorrow" SO never again after this go back to that person and say I cant do this because of Dyslexia!

Now that I had to be honest with myself it made me more open and hopefully it will do the same for you, it will make you a better happier person. I said before you can achieve the great things you want if you do what I'm suggesting. Every time you start having negative thought or ideas – try use the above technic an allow yourself to be raw and open and allow your ideas to be more positive so that your outcome are more positive.

My Dad always says to me that there nothing that bad in life to make you hate yourself so never do something that will affect your loved one or leave them behind - as I have experienced a few times in my life with friends. This may sound strong but the importance of developing the best you is being honest with you and doing this technic will help you.

Did you know that roughly 12 people (this is what has been recorded sadly it's believed its many more) a year commit suicide because of dyslexia because they have or are lying to friends family because they are ashamed and afraid of the ridicule and rejection and failing letting people down. Please, please, please never become one of these statistics. I'm showing you it's a gift it is something I'm proud of I have learnt to embrace it and actually I love the gifts its given me

Lets look at the negative and see the positive:

- I'm dyslexic and I cant read and write – negative
- Positive: because I'm dyslexic I can talk in a straightforward way and can communicate well with people. So when I'm teaching a seminar or coaching I feel I engaged with people better and listen and understand body language better.
- I didn't put ex partners first in relationship as much as should of because of this - negative

- The positive - I now have an amazing wife who know I am dyslexic and am the best man I can be to Nadine because she is number one in everything.
- I'm not with the mother of my son as feel I have let him down - negative
- Positive I feel I'm a better dad to Harry as I have had to learn from my mistakes
- I cant ride a bike wow kept this one for years negative
- Positive made me walk everywhere then jog now I love running and work as a fitness coach
- I lost a gambling bet which was £900 pound once - negative
- Positive: I very rarely bet and now never ever go against my grandad advice

I'm telling this because whatever you have in your mind-set that you think you cant ask that person on a date, application in for a job, write a book, go to college. You can. Go get a dyslexia test as a starting point don't be afraid to put your hands up and say yes I am - can you help me please. If you can do that then It has been worth opening up and sitting in front of this laptop hanging to get a break through for you.

Right so we done it we have smash the truth and are ready to go and celebrate like we score the world cup winner goal like Marco Tardelli 1982. Shouting "I'm dyslexic, I'm dyslexic and proud of it! No don't be a dick !

Right you have started and accepted which is amazing - now before you start on building you own little book of success I want you to try that tactical skill I spoke about before so imagine you are on the Titanic and you have a I min to take everything you care about into a yellow life raft before everything is lost forever - do it now this is my I min list below

- **Nadine & Kids**
- **Family**
- **Real Friends**
- **Grandad painting and war medal**
- **Gizmo ashes (not the one in gremlins – my dog)**
- **Pictures**
- **Football medals**
- **Time up I min done!**

Now look back at your list, do you see on my list I have no stress not what people think of me what people have said in the past family drama or work beliefs or me failing tests, rejection in relationship jobs all sunk all gone all at the bottom of the sea. So now you don't give a fuck - well done you actually now realise that all that matters is that you are trying be and do your best. You will forget things lose things, make mistake fail but now you have the tools and every time you start to think your not reaching or achieving your best or you are not being honest then remember that all that matters is people will respect so much more and you will see that your life will be so much better.

Chapter 7: Habits Tatctics and Skills

Webbey's rules and template for self reflections for success are listed below. Under each one I wanted you to write a one line a answer as to what its means to you. After you have done all 34 – your will see you have your own little book personally design for you with your goals, your fears, your dreams and ideas, the reasons for thing and actions to take. Trust me do this and you can look back at it every time you question any aspect of "you".

1. Know what you want.
2. Work on your gift.
3. No excuses.
4. Upgrade your values.
5. You reap what you sow.
6. Education is the great equalizer.
7. What is your dream?
8. Have boundaries for you - what are they?
9. Tell yourself the truth.
10. I dare you to fail.
11. Push through it pain don't give up.
12. Be ready to seize all opportunities.
13. Don't do it alone who can help you?
14. Do not be outworked by another in your dreams.

15. Stand up to your fears.
16. Focus on the positives outcomes.
17. Repetition, repetition, repetition.
18. Execute that idea
19. Leave your mark that day on a person, a place, a group
20. Know you are amazing
21. Don't just be an "average Joe"
22. Don't care about people who hate you or negative people
23. Set goals chunk away at your goals
24. Be driven to succeed.
25. Make a decision or choice now.
26. Find an accountability partner to help support you.
27. Believe in yourself
28. Surround yourself with high achievers and successful people - you are the average of the 5 most successful people round you - who are these?
29. Discipline yourself.
30. Have massive dreams about what you want to do
31. Build one brick at a time.

32. You don't need permission from anyone else to go for what you want.
33. Live what your talking.
34. Change your mind set.

“because I am dyslexic I am very good at finding good people who can compensate for my weaknesses

Richard Branson

“For a man to conquer himself is the first and noblest of all victories”

Plato : Greek philosopher

Reading technique :

One thing that really helped change my thinking and helped me overcome a massive fear of reading was a man called Peter James he writes great crime novel around the Brighton and Sussex area –the Roy Grace books. Peter James' style of writing and the font size really help me. He creates such easy flow in his paragraphs. He builds characters and places in the book that you get in to the rhyme of the story. The little relationships the characters have make reading the book very simple and easy. I found that if you start reading things you love or are interested in your brain will help build that repetition and recognition making the experience fun.

What really opened me up to loving books and reading (and led me to deciding to write a book - mad I know) was I tried a technic I had heard of I brought different coloured tracing paper to start I found that using yellow or blue sometimes red and orange paper and putting over the page just open up the page and can really help involve me into the book I didn't lose track and it helped almost set the mood of that chapter or page. Seriously try it I know it sound crazy but there have been studies that have shown how colour helps people with dyslexia focus and engage. I was sceptical to start but its really works. Try it – give it a go and email me to let me know how you get on (email at the back of the book) I would love to hear how feel once you have done it and if you managed to get lost in a book as I now do.

I have an aim every year to read at least 12 books 1 a month so in five years (shit more math's) I would have read 60 books! Yep – 60! if someone would had said to me I would read 60 books in my life time I would of said they were taking the piss! Image the knowledge and things you could discover if you just try - so finish this book your have 59 left happy days!

Dyslexia glasses:

Now you think I'm joking but I'm serious. I started with colour tinted overlays and it made such a huge different to my reading. I used to get bad headaches and my eyes would hurt when I tried to read for prolonged times. I would find myself exhausted and wanting to sleep after just a couple of pages as you can image not great in a class or a lecture! So I had yellow tinted overlays it really improved my reading and helped me read for longer periods. Another tool that made me fall in love with reading even more. Its amazing to think something as simple as a tint to lenses made such a difference. You can get all different colours it about finding the right one for you. Colour options:

- Mint green
- Blue
- Yellow
- Rose
- Purple

You need to go and see a specialist optician. I visited a company called Cerium Visual Technologies and they put me in touch with a company in Guildford call the Eye Academy.

Spelling techniques:

I have find spelling and will always find it the hardest challenge in terms of explaining to others in my work and personal life. Funny story - when I met my partner I charmed her with my Hollywood good looks (obviously) and my chat ha-ha - no seriously I find engaging face to face with people so much better for me I feel I can read peoples body language and tone fair better and engage with anyone. I feel this has helped me a lot in life business and with client's overtime. Anyway after getting my partners number I was struggling to express myself and explain stuff over text and understand what she was saying back to me. For nearly two weeks I struggled and honestly thought she wouldn't go on a date with me and it wouldn't get started and someone else would take her breath away (Berlin Top Gun film - bang got it in somewhere) I did tell her from the start that I was Dyslexic. I don't know if this counts as some type of Cilla Black dating tip but the boy/ girl whatever they are - from the off tell them because if there really interested in you they will stay and understand. If not it's their loss. Like I've told you, you are amazing, any person reading this book you are a small percentage in the word that want to improve their life and the lives of others around them - anyway off track - once I explained the struggle - I was asking her "so what have you ever done or achieved that your proud of" she said "I've got my *diving* licence" so I replied with "oh that great so what car do you drive? or like driving?" what a numpty! Seriously how did I pull this one off with that chat?!

So the technic – back to the use of colours - but this time I suggest for your self or a child or student using colours has to be a huge help with development the brain can slow its pattern down for colours but also association by colours is a massive building block for painting pictures or memory in the brain to trigger a point, word, action or feeling for us. So buy a small mini white board and different set of colours and you can workout phonics and de-coding words that will help you understand but believe me well really help in lots of different aspect of learning and life. Example:

light

might

night

now by just colouring in the common phonic sounds in words I always put picture that remind me of that word to help associate to that then by chunking this way and thses colours make it easier to see.

Planner and Organisation : Dan Meredith

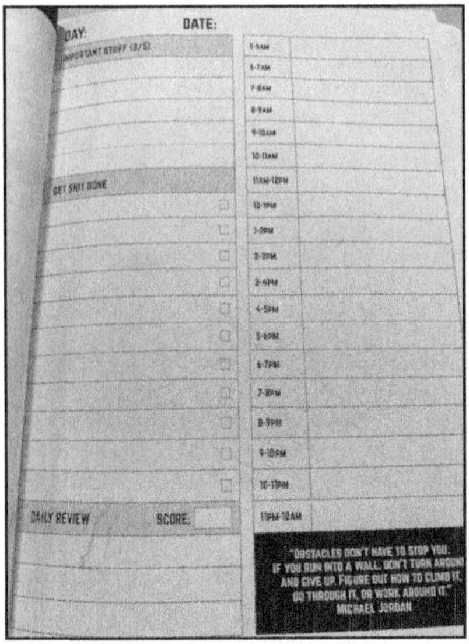

As I've said dyslexics have terrible focus. However, since I read his book and design my own style of planning its really helped me. Having a planner is so important it will help you stay on track and get things done. Make it a game for your self for instance put 5 task down you must do that day and make task 6 a reward then every time you do this you get a reward - it honestly works. If you have children or you coach try this style see what results you get. I hope this will help you.

Breaking or pushing the rules

So its was 19th October 2005 - I was working on the railway as a signalling engineer at Waterloo station. All day my mate at work were saying about going to the Chelsea v Real Bertis Champion League game that night (as Waterloo station is just couple of stops from Stamford bridge). NOW what I'm going to say is again what a lot of this book is about, I'm telling you what <u>not</u> to do. You'll understand why at the end - so as a Chelsea fan I wanted to go. My mate suggested that there would be tickets on sale at the stadium. As we arrive and I'm queuing up with him even through he has a ticket and we are getting closer (I'm about 3 people from the front I see the ticket box says "Sold Out". I was thinking bollocks got a long train trip back and now wasted 40 min for nothing! Then out of the corner of my eye I see a gate into the ground disability access, we look at each other my mate told me to shut up there was no way that it was going to work! I thought fuck it I'll try as all ready out of luck at the ticket office so didn't have anything to lose. So we go walking up arms locked together like we were on a first date! I don't know why we did this looked like idiots! I go up to the steward and my mate say excuses me I'm the carer for this lad and I have one ticket but he seem to have lost his I'm so sorry the steward reminded me of Greg Davis the comedian he said what wrong with him? My mate said ermm he's got dyslexia acting like he was bloody Tom Cruise and I was Dustin Hoffman in Rain Man. Greg the steward said that not a disability and turn round to a another steward who was and looked scarily like a fatter Micky Flanagan and he looked like it was his first day – he started looking down at a list and look back at Greg and said yeah it is mate actually! The whistle had just gone for the game and Greg looked at us and nods go in! What a result I'm pissing myself inside and we get to sit in some one the best seats in the ground Chelsea won the game 4-0 Drogba, Carvalho, Joe Cole, Crespo scored. It's so bad that in 2005 I used this but it was worth it just this once.

Chapter 8:
Coaching

"our success has not been years of winning but years of devastating setbacks how we handle and learn from this is what makes as a overnight success"

Bobby Robson England Manager, Barcelona

I know for a fact and for you as a teacher, coach or parent will need to understand is that a child or adult with dyslexia will forgot skills that they have appear to mastered more quickly that others if they don't practice (see Chapter 3). Often coaches would come up to me and say that child seemed to have learnt this now few weeks later has lost the knowledge/skill. To you it will seem as if the child has forgotten or can't be bothered, is lazy or lacks effort but it's really not that. It's the basic fact that he or she is working x10 harder to retain information and will lose the information if they do not practice the same. I'm going to give you few ideas or how to overcome this from each club I worked with I extracted ideas that I believe depending on what angle you are coming from in this section will help you develop the child , players, children and most importantly in this section you not progressing yourself it will show you how can you help people with dyslexia become the best vision of themselves.

I do apologise if you are not a sports fan but the habits and tip from my experiences in this world have truly help me in other aspect of my life and others so it does work!

Extracting the little gems of practices I have seen or created myself can really help progress you in your career in coaching or as a parent frustrated you can't help you son or daughter. As well this what we all want in life is to try and develop ourselves and others this is pure fact and from early in the WHYS in this book (see above chapters).

Brentford fc:

My time at Brentford was one of the biggest moments in my coaching life. I was lucky enough to be in the Brentford environment at a critical time when I believe Brentford Academy was probably one of the best academies in the country. There are some amazing coaches there now who have gone on to do some great things with other clubs and it's a sad thing that the academy went. At the time I met a man called Colin Brown. Now, Colin didn't know at the time, but, I was only a level 1 coach trying to work my way up, but, I met him on a module two course through the FA. Colin was so open and helpful there, he said to me I could come up to one of Brentford's development centres up at Northolt, which is for me was about a 55-minute drive just up past Heathrow. I used to go up there, taking my work van, (which was obviously naughty). I used to drive there for nothing and volunteer and it's one of the first things that I'm going to kind of help you (pearl of wisdom) if you are someone who's trying to get somewhere like I've put in the book before, volunteering and getting yourself in there is one of the best ways you can turn to develop yourself in the area that you want to be in. Just keep turning up every week, ask people questions, keep learning about the thing that you want to, get a mentor, get someone that's going to help you. That's what I did when I was at Brentford. I used all the coaches that were there and used all their different experiences to help me develop in to the coach I am today.

One of the biggest lessons of being in that development centre and being at Brentford, was the club had a few things that I can really take out of it that I'll give you in this book. First thing is for a coach, teacher or parents:

Repetition is massive and intensity. Brentford's probably one of the only clubs that I've worked at where everything was in an intense environment and they were working hard against other clubs. They didn't have technically the best players, but they worked it to their advantage, they brought players in that would work for Brentford, and I think that was one of the biggest keys. With the job I got to work with the players in this environment and I went to development centres to learn more skills. I worked hard, I put my time and effort in. I learnt off other coaches. On a Saturday I would go to the academy and I would sit there and help out other coaches and just keep working away and you'd get more respect, more opportunities.

Before long, I was helping different age groups. I was helping take little groups to sessions, and I started working with under 9's, under 12's, all these different groups and started doing trial games for the club, I kept pushing and pushing myself. One of the only things that Brentford did that no other club did it when I worked and also when I was learning as a coach and I still use to this day as well, is pure honesty. It's one of the only clubs that after a development centre night, after a game, after trials, people would come in for 6-12 weeks and we'd sit down in a changing room and we would pick the players that would stay and players that would go. It was ruthless in all honesty, but you had to learn to fight your corner.

What I appreciated most was that Brentford coaches were not afraid to be argumentative and say exactly what was on their mind during meetings. Their abilities to challenge, accepted norms, brought values to a lot of the conversations we had. The best coaches, I believe, are direct and candid. Fairness is something different, everyone cannot be treated the same, but, fairness is understood by the team and where this is completely open. Nothing undermines team morale more than dishonest head coaches or leaders, and if there is no honesty there is no trust and without it, fairness becomes the issue, with staff or with players complaining behind your back. You had to fight your corner everyone was brutal with you. Brutal honesty was best and I've now taken this into some of my coaching through the years that you have to be honest with people.

Outcome for coaches /teachers/parents: be honest with them don't lie to make out they are improving if they are not. Be approachable to dyslexics and be patience take you time to understand them and don't be unfair or judge the person and once you help them you will get the respect and reward back out of it

Benfica :

I was on a level 2 coaching course down in Worthing in West Sussex and it was absolutely pissing it down with rain, and this is where I met a good friend of mine, Georgie Gomez. Georgie had come over from Portugal to do his coaching badge as he wanted to develop his skills as the FA were credited as one of the best and at the time, Portugal didn't really have too many coaching courses. So, Georgie invited me over talking and we went to the training.

What I found out was interesting, was Georgie was the first-ever coach I'd met that was dyslexic as well. While the course was going on, Georgie and I would discuss for ages about his coaching methods, what he wanted to achieve, how he felt that his coaching skills were improving and how he saw things that would make a huge difference. We talked about dyslexia as well, and about how we felt it helped us become better coaches. He taught me a lot.

I'm going to give you one greatest lessons that Georgie taught me and when I was at the facilities: The average persons attention span is only 11 seconds which is why consistency and the messages have to be key when you are coaching.

As I was watching Georgie from the stands as he was teaching and training with the other academy coaches, I noticed something very different. Georgie had a tiny little tactic board in his pocket and he would bring a player over every 10-15 seconds out of the group and he'd explain something very quickly on the board and they'd go back out. It was a great thing that I've taken from this, which, obviously, I'm going give to you, is that one of the learning styles that will help players with dyslexia when they're in your teams, is to have that visual image in their pocket. It was such a small little tactic board, but it made a huge difference. Georgie could explain to players very quickly and very precisely what role they needed or what they needed to do, he could do it in a way that he hardly needed to say anything, he just drew a little diagram with small little markers on a little tactic board and the players understood. And you can do this in any aspect of your life,

Outcome for coaches /teachers/parents: use an example, use a piece of paper, use toys, use something a tactic board that will engage that person and they can see this visual learning style

Brighton & Hove Albion :

At Brighton Football Club, I found great coaches and friends that I'm still friends with today. Also, it was the first club that I'd been with where I had the opportunity to be free and express some of my own coaching styles and how I wanted to develop the players. Also, it was the first time at a club that I'd met a player called Marcus Puddephatt. As I looked down my list for the new players for the season that I was getting for my under 11's squad, the players have their names on the side and, obviously, if they've got any issues, normally they have asthma or something written down that they might need, it was the first time down on a piece of paper as I looked down at a young player called Marcus had dyslexia.

It intrigued me as obviously being dyslexic myself and one of my first experiences in football to see how the player would adapt to some of my ideas. So, as I did the roll call for the first session together. I saw who Marcus was and I started looking at the ways he was working. Marcus was a good little player, he had raw speed and talent, but he'd either take his time or always go too fast when doing something.

I'd noticed some trait of myself looking at Marcus as a young player and I realized that maybe I was overloading with information. So, I started using some of the things that I thought would help him.

One of them for a start was breaking things down and using colours. So, for example, instead of explaining when I was using the whole group to show a demo, I'd then pull Marcus out a little bit to the side and go through something similar of what I wanted to achieve or get him to watch me. As the session went on to see the 3d pictures in reality , but, also do it with coloured cones. I noticed that when I started doing it with the coloured cones and broke it down for Marcus that all he needed to do is get to the red cone, to the yellow cone and out. Instead of explaining the whole concept of what I was trying to get through to him. He could do it and he'd done it brilliantly when he took his time and he thought about it and used the sequence that I'd give him like a road map. Marcus then got into the squad I was taken to Holland and he was one of the best players in the whole tournament .

Brighton was the first squad that I'd worked with where we went on a tour and into a tournament in Holland and where I fell in love with more of the Dutch game than I had, had previously. One of our first experiences was a club called De Graafschap. Now, with, I had the under 11's squad and the under 11's for them was also the manager was the academy director as well. As I sat in his office drinking coffee and we discussed football and ours views. We sat with a Subbuteo size board going through tactics and game strategies and out come for that days game. One of the things that really sunk in when we kind of had the same understanding of the game and what we love was that he said something to me that stuck. He said to me "being a good coach or a teacher doesn't just depend on what you have to say. Think about that you listen and you listen to the different learning styles that a child prefers at adapting and observing. I gave one player who you could see was a lot of detail and give another player broader guidelines."

I also noticed when they gave the players accountability and responsibility in the sense that the players at that academy, would start doing the first 10 minutes of the session. When we spoke about it, he told me that every week a new player did it, but, he'd give the players freedom and understanding to start building their own sessions and making it more enjoyable and more engaging for them.

Whilst in my first year over in Holland, me and my other coach at the time were working on.... I wanted to invest in the players' development and gave them a roles that they could achieve, i.e. below.

Player 1 would wake all players up for breakfast. Player 2 make sure all players had their kit on and all the same kit on when they're downstairs. Player 3 to put all the plates away after the food in the kitchen. Players 4, 5, 6 and 7would get all the rooms cleaned and everyone get ready for training. Player 8 training kit and all boots would be sorted. Player 9 make sure all players have water bottles with them, spare ones. Player 10 to act as a captain in the sessions so everyone would listen. Player 11 to help put all the equipment away correctly after training and so on with the squad. But, by doing this, we help them not become entitled, complacent or lazy and develop accountability for them while they're away from their parents.

Outcome for coaches /teachers/parents: from a dyslexic point of view, I think giving one simple task a day can help them achieve something every day, would make a huge difference to their lives. Also give them input into the lesson or session let them feel there have a little bit of control or what's happening and invested and your see how much more engagement you will receive

Arsenal FC:

Working for arsenal was a great experience under Barry Jeffries and Daniel Sault I feel that there was one of the most organise but most technical club I worked with they gave me a whole manual and week to week topic I must do with the players philosophy and culture Under 9's & Under 10's, for example below this was in 2014:

Warm Up for Each Week - Ball Manipulation (turning, dribbling, changing direction)

Week 1: Short Passing and Receiving & Possession (back foot receiving and play forward)

Week 2: Quick Passing with a Finish & Possession (back foot receiving and play forward)

Week 3: 2 v 2 & 3 v 3 (Attack) & Possession (back foot receiving and play forward)

Week 4: Shooting and Volleying & Possession (back foot receiving and play forward)

Week 5: Arial Control & Possession (back foot receiving and play forward)

Week 6: Quick Passing with a Finish & Possession (back foot receiving and play forward)

Week 7: 2 v 2 & 3 v 3 (Defence) & Possession (back foot receiving and play forward)

Week 8: Short Passing and Receiving & Possession (back foot receiving and play forward)

Week 9: Quick Passing with a Finish & Possession (back foot receiving and play forward)

I found that my skill improve as a coach and that with Arsenal you could bring your coaching style in but add in to their philosophy. The club with very big on feedback after every session and before session you would discuss plans and also back up plan for numbers of players or adapting to different age groups. Feedback was massive I always felt I was developing as a coach and being push to improve all the time, standards were high and expectations on you as a coach to be the best in your age group I found that being organised was so important for the players outcome in games and training. It gave them real purpose and belief in what we was trying to achieve.

The transition in to the next week session and homework I would set them really showed when the next week they couldn't wait to show me the skills I had taught them the week before. I would of loved to stay at the club at the time but other commitments were far more important (little tip) life balance like earlier with the Dan Meredith organise break your days down into who and what needs the time.

Outcome for coaches /teachers/parents: get feedback from the group or child or the lesson or practice so very import for you to help them in their long term plan. Also when working with the person with dyslexia give them feedback all the time I believe it will help their progress and development knowing they are on the right path. Giving a person with dyslexia clear instructions in what there are achieving will also help them concentrate on what you are currently doing. As I said in chapter three dyslexics can see the end goal but can't put all the dots together to achieve the end goal be the support the person that can connect the dots for them.

Sampdoria FC :

Being here in Genoa in Italy was one of my life dreams from being a little boy watching Channel 4 Italian football with James Richardson and Peter Brackley's voices talking about favourite teams and legends like Pagliuca, Lombardo ,Gullit, Vialli. I arrived at the Genoa airport and waited for Giovanni who was a brilliant bloke. I had emailed him about visiting the club I didn't think I would hear anything back but I sent an email, then just before Christmas (Italian football has a break at this time) I received a email telling me to come over.

When at the training ground Giovanni explain to be the philosophy at the time was about recovery of players, lifestyles, regeneration and restoration. This is the first time that it really hit me how many areas and people were involved in academy football. Then just the TTPP model used which develop players on the tactical, technical, psychological and psychical elements. My few days there were eyes openers and really helped to develop me as a coach. Something that struck me on my last day when I was in the players toilet's - there was messages all over the wall on laminated paper, when I went back in to Giovanni office I asked him what was on these and he told me they were changed every week had motivational message and details of things there had worked on that week it really help sink things in. In that moment there was nothing else the players were doing or thinking about (always nice to have something to read when in the loo!). I've been back since and actually coached in the development and academy set up which I loved. The players where brilliant and made my coaching development far greater than I could of imagined.

Outcome for coaches /teachers/parents: from this experience what I believe you can use is - firstly look at the environment you are creating before teaching is it relaxed will it help inspire your pupils or children? Secondly try to put a word just one word they are practicing in you toilet for dyslexic's to practice or whatever they are studying that week. Alternate this with a positive message when doing there business trust me little shift in habits go a long way. Finally let them relax and recover don't think that doing extra hours will improve, remember it is never going away they are always going be dyslexic so relax show them how to relax and not worry and over a long period time and with the fun element within their learning they will get there .

FA COURSES:

I was on a development course with the FA and I got to met a late and great coach who I look up to and inspired me as coach, one of my coaching idols Don Howe.

Don was behind the success of some great achievement in English football like Wimbledon 1988 victory, England 1990 World Cup and under Terry Venables in Euro 96. During my short time with him I asked him what advice he could give me. Don look at me and said "Focus on always delivering and rehearse it, the goal of a session is not just to do the session it's to perform everything must be aimed at perfecting the delivery - this is why great players and team competition is the iron to sharpen the sword".

Other coaches that I found that made a real different to my development was Ted Dale, Ted has a brilliant way of breaking down detail and painting the picture you want to created ted also has very good inter personal skills there are so good in term of how he help me with as a coach and the support work, plus paperwork in the coaching world . Another coach is Andy

Ritchie who was my tutor on my youth module course. This was a great course to go on and helped me understand each phase of a child's development. What Andy did, which I haven't seen in any other coach do, was he could make any session into brilliant game where you didn't realise you was actually achieving the outcome he had set out to achieve. He had so many different games, ideas making every session fun enjoyable.

I've had the pleasure of spending time with is Nick Levett, he was the head of the FA National Game for Youth Development. Nick was so accurate and articulate when delivering session and explaining he could create different environments with his tonality. I found him brilliant in understanding children and developing and looking from different angles working with diverse groups. I found when speaking once to Nick how engaging he was with young players and actually knew small details about the player which would dictate how he would approached a session with them.

Outcome for coaches /teachers/parents: when with a dyslexic person or group design and think about how you are going to deliver the lesson how you going get the most out of it for them also how you structure and break down the session or lesson or homework. Make it fun for them and they will not realise they are working hard and learning at the same time - created games to learn.

NON LEAGUE FOOTBALL

I love non-league football for the pure fact that if you've got things that you want to create, you have the opportunity to do that if you get the opportunity to be in a club. One of mine was at Three Bridges Football Club. They're playing currently in the South League, Isthmian league to others. I was the head coach for the under 21's, which basically was the reserves at the time. A few of the first team players would come and train with us as well. What I did there, which I really believe worked, I achieved two cup semi-finals and a third-place only behind Maidstone and Woking at the time with players of around 16/17 years old in an under 21 squad, was helping them create scenarios, painting pictures in their head. I believe I made them diverse and created ways of setting coaching sessions to offer them mind-sets and help them develop their mind craft.

I used to play games without the rules or I used to implement little different things, like, for example, I would play rugby rule styles where they couldn't pass forward. I'd put Aussie rules in there as well, where they could get, pick the ball up and kick it up the field. I used blocking like in the NFL. Using these ideas, I felt was giving the players to think outside of the box, making them adaptability, developing their decision-making skills, taking upon themselves and putting them out of their comfort zone. The unorthodox games I played helped improved and develop their vision.

Outcome for coaches /teachers/parents: You must adapt to the changes and embrace it. Don't always teach the same style, tonality. This will help dyslexics accept this success and help them adapt to unforeseen circumstances i.e. moving school, classes, clubs and jobs. Looking for fun ways to think outside the box. Help develop a growth mind-set to a new environment.

Working with senior players and non-league players is to get them players to ask questions and give you feedback. I feel is one of the best ways to be non-clinical and involved and open-ended questions to help during sessions. I believe it's down to you to make sessions in class or homework effective. I designed after a practice a warm-up that lasted about 19 minutes on the pitch to help perform the best. You should be trying this.

To teach the players anything new before they take the field, instead of you just going over the basics of the game plan one last time and keeping interaction with the players to a minimum. The last thing they need is a bunch of surplus information floating around their head as they are trying to get ready to compete. Keep it simple and brief at all times.

"Educating the mind without educating the heart is no education at all"

Aristotle

CHELSEA FC :

I had a short spell at Chelsea at this time one of the biggest lesson I took out of this was to give the players more creative licences. I wanted the player to understand that making mistake and trying new things was good and you can learn so much more. One of my focus' from the style I wanted to create as a coach was to always build and improve relationships as a coach. I played with the different styles of teacher from militant to neglectful, to permissive to authoritative but with each style I was adjusting the warmth scale of caring for the players to build a winning relationship with players in all the above areas in this chapter you must find your own style, not coping not being a robot but the real you. I found at Chelsea using my style as a human being and personal qualities I created effective learning but being authoritative but very caring and warm to each individual player their needs I also used to share something about myself to the players after each session which in turn open trust and you receive information back it was never football related but once you create trust and care and give them the opportunity to ask lots of question you open the door to a new world of development .

Outcome for coaches /teachers/parents: Be a role model for the dyslexic person give them a person to inspire to. Show them that its good for making mistake and to learn from them and give them the freedom to be the real them show them the real you and crated your learning styles and you can open the door for them. If you're a parent then tell your child something they don't know about yourself and you'll find out so much more about them.

Final outcome

from me: Identity is a funny thing. When you think your life has defined you, or you've defined yourself, there's always another challenge or another chapter. It's all about getting outside of your own comfort zone. Until you do, you'll never know what you're capable of.

"You will never reach your destination if you stop and throw stones at every dog that barks"

Jose Mourinho

CHAPTER 9:
Interviews

Jo Bradley -founder of learning with dyslexia

My journey into the world of dyslexia first started 30 years ago when I started working with children. I noticed that some children within my care found learning Nursery Rhymes and literacy skills challenging to pick up and I wondered why. It wasn't until I started teaching a class of Year 1 students that I realised that certain children found reading and writing incredibly difficult to grasp and that they didn't learn in the conventional way. However, no one gave any advice of how to best support these children. It wasn't until I met my husband in 2001 that I began to truly start my journey into the world of dyslexia. My husband was verbally articulate and knew a lot about science and design- I found him fascinating to spend time with. However, I noticed that he would avoid writing and never read for pleasure. It wasn't until we went on holiday to Italy and we were writing postcards to family and friends that I had written at least 10 and Mark was still on his first postcard. He had described everything as being 'lovely'- the food is lovely, having a lovely time, lovely hotel. When I asked him about this, he said that he confidently knew how to spell the word 'lovely' and that's why he had used it to describe his experiences.

At the time I had a gorgeous little boy in my Year 1 class who was finding reading and writing very challenging and his mother had sent him for a formal diagnosis- he was diagnosed with dyslexia. This was really the first time that I was really aware of dyslexia. I sent Mark for an assessment with a local organisation and he was formally diagnosed at the age of 29 years old. His mum described how she had been told his Year 1/2 teacher that he was slow and retarded and definitely not dyslexic. After his assessment, Mark felt a great sense of relief and we could then build on his strengths and I could support his weaknesses. For example, administrative tasks.

A Full Diagnostic Assessment

If your child is struggling with aspects of literacy, like reading and writing, then assessment can often be the first step to understanding the obstacles that are getting in the way of your child's progress. It can be the key to unlocking their talents and self-belief. A diagnostic assessment takes 3-4 hours and can be a very tiring and intensive experience My Learning with Dyslexia assessments are not 'tests' that give a yes/no answer; they are focused on understanding a child as an individual and on finding a positive way forward. The reports aim to be helpful, clear, and easy to read and understand. They contain recommendations on how best your child learns and how they can improve their future 'lived experiences'. All of my assessments are followed up by practical advice in a written report.

I am in a very privileged position as I get to spend high quality time with individuals who can be experiencing feelings of failure within our education system, in their workplace, and in society. When I write a report, I am mindful that the information and guidance within the report can shape an individual's future and mental health and wellbeing. I aim to report the facts in a sensitive and caring way. I aim to write reports that are easy to understand for both individuals, parents and educators. I give an overview of the tests that I carry out, observations and results. I give clear recommendations within areas of learning that individuals may find challenging within their lives, education settings or in the workplace. I am a teacher, and I totally understand and empathise with the huge workload that teachers within our classrooms experience on a daily basis. Therefore, I aim to give recommendations that are easy to implement and that don't cost the earth, but that can, and do, make a huge difference to the children's experiences of learning within their environments.

I also assess many adults who have returned to study or who are struggling within the workplace, or life. It's never too late to be diagnosed- I had a lovely 23 years old young man who came to visit me who was a non-reader. It took a lot of courage for him to contact me and to come for lessons, but he did it and flourished. Once he was able to read a whole new world opened up to him, which was once blocked. He was able to book himself a flight and go travelling across the USA and Australia- he fell in love and now lives very happily in Australia with his new wife, and I have a acquired his dog! Who is adorable and a happy addition to our family.

What does an assessment involve?

Full Diagnostic Assessment

Aims to identify – or diagnose - what is at the root of the difficulties that are causing concern. A Learning with Dyslexia Specialist Assessor's assessment is usually appropriate for persons over 5 years old who have not previously been assessed, or for those who require a full update on progress since a previous assessment. The assessment will usually take 3 to 4 hours.

Full Diagnostic Assessment Package- £425.00

A full diagnostic assessment involving a range of tests is carried out and a comprehensive and detailed assessment report is produced, including a diagnosis of dyslexia if, and when appropriate.

Each assessment report will include:

- Summary of assessment report findings
- Summary of background information from home and school/college, including history of support at school/college based on information given in your questionnaire
- Detailed interpretation of test results, including:
    - General Underlying Ability
    - Attainments, e.g. reading, spelling, writing
    - Cognitive processing skills, e.g. memory, phonological awareness, speed of phonological processing
    - Basic mathematical skills
    - Handwriting skills, e.g. legibility, speed
- Conclusion – a holistic view of assessment findings
- Table of test scores
- Essential recommendations for supporting the learner where relevant:
    - At home
    - In the classroom
    - Access arrangements in exams
    - Specialist teacher/tutor
    - Full details of all the tests used in the session will be included for reference.
    - Suggestions for Access Arrangements in examinations will be included if appropriate.

A diagnostic assessment costs £425, which is an investment, and I am aware that it is not financially viable for some families, which saddens me. Each assessment takes me between 3-5 hours and I then take another 4-8 hours marking and writing up the assessment report. I wish that there was more funding available so that every person who needed an assessment could gain access to one.

Q1 When did you know realise you or you son had dyslexia?
My son, Jacob, never crawled- he went straight to walking at 9 months of age. He was very physically active but slower to talk than his peers. He enjoyed Reception class and learning through play. In 2010 when my son started Year 1, I noticed that he started to struggle with literacy and was unable to read any of the basic words being sent home on flashcards or in his reading books. Fear, worry and anxiety crept into my mind. After talking to his teachers about my concerns they suggested that he would catch up and that he was still very young, but I knew that my son was intelligent and verbally able and that something was wrong. Yet, I didn't know how best to support his future learning needs and ensure that he became able to read and write like his friends in the class. He adored listening to me read and loved telling stories. He was extremely verbally articulate but was then unable to get his ideas down onto paper. My husband's mother described that Mark had been just like this as a boy and I realised that Jacob was probably dyslexic like his dad. This is when I took my

first steps to learning how to best support dyslexic learners by researching best practise teaching methods to support dyslexic learners and enrolling myself on the Postgraduate Certificate in Dyslexia and Literacy course through Dyslexia Action. As soon as I qualified as a Specialist dyslexia and literacy teacher, I began teaching my son and some of his peers, who were also struggling to read and write. Through just a 1-hour session each week the children regained their confidence in their ability to learn, their self-esteem flourished and they were soon reading, writing and smiling once again.

My daughter, who thrived in her Reception class at school, became disenchanted in Year 1 as she struggled to keep up with her friends and she just couldn't understand why she couldn't read and write as well as them. Her teacher also advised that she would catch up, but of course she didn't. As she struggled more at school her confidence plummeted and she became more disengaged and behavioural problems started. I assessed her and of course she is dyslexic too.

Q2 Can you tell us a time in your life experience it really affects you ?

My husband Mark has answered these-

Whenever I have to do administration tasks, like ordering something from somebody and having to put all of my personal details onto a form. Answering an email that is going to be longer than a paragraph or 100+ words in length.

(My friend's son, Joshua, answered questions in blue)
When I see a large amount of wording on a page, I find it difficult to read, as it seems overwhelming.

Q3 what about a time you think it help you out?
I don't really know- but I suppose my boat, my Pedalo that I'm designing and making from scratch. I'm creating a model in my mind of the part imaging where the stresses may be where its going to be in compression and tension and prepare layers of carbon glass to provide enough strength but minimising use of material and weight.

I find puzzles easy as I think my dyslexic brain helps me to figure them out.

Q4 any silly funny story that you think feel dyslexia contributed to it?
I've recently moved into my first ever office instead of assessing and teaching from my home, which is super amazing. My students love the new space and so do I! When the new signage was put up outside my office saying 'Learning with Dyslexia' one of my 6-year-old students asked her mum a serious question. "What is Jo's real name? I thought that it was Jo Bradley?" Her mum looked confused and when her daughter pointed to the sign she realised why. "I know that doesn't say Jo Bradley, so what is her name?" Her mum explained that it was my company name.

My 12-year-old daughter was writing a book review and wrote 'the story had loads of 'twits' in it instead of 'twists'. We both laughed about that spelling faux pas!

Q5 any routine, habits, tactics you use to overcome day to day tasks?
General avoidance or ask partner to do things for me. Use Smartphone to record notes, reminders, check spellings, read messages.

I take photos of the board at school to help me remember things, for homework or revision. I also ask Alexa or Siri to spell words for me and to tell me interesting facts.

Q6 what your dream idea of what you want to achieve from learning with dyslexia company
Every day I am driven by the amazing people that I have the good fortune to work with. The more time that I spend with my students, parents and educators the more apparent it becomes that my role is a valuable one. I have just moved out of my home, where I have been working for over 7 years, and into my first ever office, which I am loving. I finally feel ready to take the next big leap with my business. I have come to the realisation that I can only reach a small number of people who are local to me and that I need to broaden my horizons. I teach over 20 students a week on a 121 basis and often assess 1 or 2 people a week. I regularly speak to worried parents about my experiences of working and

supporting people with dyslexia and find myself repeating similar advice many times. My brother has recently moved into the area from London and he has a background in Post Production, so with his help and guidance I am going to make a series of videos with advice and support for parents and teachers. I aim to run training events for parents and educators, and with the support of others in education put some training for teachers together- I'd love to travel around the UK, and who knows maybe the rest of the world. I'm going to use some of my dyslexic students 'outside the box' thinking skills to reach and help more people. I'm aiming to complete my Masters degree in Dyslexia and Specific Learning Difficulties with Bath Spa University by January 2021, and then start writing books of tips and strategies for parents on practical ways to support their dyslexic child. There is also a book burgeoning inside me bursting to get out for teachers on simple practical strategies on how to spot and best support dyslexic students within the learning environment.

Q7 if you could put in or change something in the special needs education system what would you implement to help develop young people with dyslexia.?

I would implement training for all Head teachers, teachers and support assistants on how to recognise and support students with dyslexia and other Specific Learning Difficulties. I know that when I was training for a 4-year degree in Education I only had a 2-hour session on dyslexia. Unfortunately, I don't think this has changed much over the past 20 years. I recently gave some inset training to a large group of secondary school teachers and it became very apparent that these teachers had little awareness of how dyslexia affects students in their classrooms and how they can best support them to learn in their classrooms. It made me think of the Hamlyn car manuals and how I should write a simple one for teachers on how to care for a dyslexic student. For example, limit the amount of copying from the board and have a 'volunteer reading policy' instead of making every child read aloud in their class. The charity 'Made by Dyslexia' has some superb training on dyslexia and how to support a dyslexic child/adult. It includes the use of Assistive Technology (AT), which I am extremely passionate about. I am currently writing my Masters degree dissertation about using AT to support writing. The use of AT can be the key to unlocking writing potential in a student if they use 'speech to text' facility. I have experienced the joy of seeing students eyes light up when they get introduced to the speech to text facility on Word- suddenly they can get all of their amazing ideas and thoughts down onto a page without worrying about their spellings. They can then become independent learners as the computer can then read their work back to them by using the text to speech facility. This allows students to edit their work all by themselves giving them ownership of their learning- its magic!

Q8 as a parent with or with not child or children with dyslexia what advice would you give to others?
It can be extremely worrying as a parent to see your child struggle to grasp literacy skills and to watch them become disenchanted with school and learning. Initially, I would raise any concerns with my child's teacher and the school SENCo and find out what help or support there is available for my child. Most parents have a deep knowing about their own children, so don't be put off if your child's teacher is dismissive- keep persevering and become your child's voice and advocate. When I initially approached my children's teachers, I was told that they were still young and that they would catch up- they never did. I was extremely lucky as there was a Specialist dyslexia teacher, Bev, who lived locally to me and who supported other children at their school, so I approached her for advice. I learned so many 'pure gold nuggets' of information from that dear teacher. I will always remember the time that she said to my son, 'Do you know what Jacob, when I got out my cereal packet this morning it didn't say you can read this because you're only on a yellow book band. When I got in my car and drove to school the road signs didn't say, Bev, you can't read this because you're not a free reader. Jacob you can choose to read whatever you want to read and if I was you, I would choose to read everything that I find interesting.' I would highly recommend visiting the PATOSS website and finding a specialist dyslexia teacher and assessor who lived near me and

phoning them for advice and support. I think early diagnosis is key to unlocking a child's potential.With over 10 years of specialising in supporting dyslexic students I now have a much deeper understanding of how they can and do learn. Specialist teaching really does work. I absolutely love teaching a non-reader to read.

Q9 if you had a choice who would you like to be for one day? And why?
I really admire the singer Paloma Faith. I love her music, her vibrant personality and the way that she performs on stage. I have seen her perform several times live and her costumes, energy and presence on stage is electrifying. I would love to be able to sing but my voice leaves a lot to be desired! It is only fit for my shower, not Wembley stadium! The thought of singing and dancing on stage would fill me with dread and just for one day I would love to have the confidence and skills to be able to shine! Paloma talks about real life, good and bad experiences. My children and I can relate to the words and sentiments in her songs. Of course, she is also dyslexic and being her for a day would allow me to truly experience what a dyslexic mind experiences every day.

Q10 who is your role model?
I have great admiration for Kate Griggs, who is the Founder and CEO of the amazing charity 'Made by Dyslexia'. She is a huge advocate for dyslexia and strives to highlight the importance of the skills that dyslexics bring to our world and how they should be nurtured and embraced as an asset and necessity. I

love the fact that she encourages every adult to place dyslexia as a strength on their CV. She aims to change others perceptions of dyslexia and show how dyslexic minds process information differently. A dyslexic has divergent, lateral thinking that has created some of the world's greatest inventions, brands and art. Yet dyslexia is still perceived as a disadvantage. She highlights the fact that our schools aren't designed for dyslexic thinking, stating that most teachers aren't trained in dyslexia, meaning most dyslexic kids are unidentified and unsupported. She aims to create solutions by working with experts and strategic partners to develop campaigns, films & tools to explain and support dyslexia. She has launched CONNECTING THE DOTS, a global advocacy campaign and movement with one mission; to level the playing-field so every dyslexic can achieve their potential. Wow! What an amazing woman!

Q11 what have you find is your biggest struggle with dyslexia ?

I'm not going to lie- living with 3 dyslexics can challenging at times. I find that I have to be super organised when we go anywhere as inevitably my family will forget key items. We are usually always late as our combined time keeping skills are poor! When the children were young, I helped to write checklists of things that we needed to take to school and both children had their own places for their shoes, coats and school things. Patience is key- every day my family and my students amaze and excite me. I love the fact that my children can now see their dyslexia as a 'gift'.

Larry May

Clubs played for: Leicester City, Barnsley, Sheffield Wednesday, Brighton (1976-1988).And was in the **1986–87 Football League Second Division PFA Team of the Year** after this Larry went on as a youth coach at Brighton and Portsmouth, was a PE teacher in a special needs school, then became football development officer for Crawley Council before becoming coaching development manager for the Surrey FA and was football development officer at Brighton I interview Larry while in Portugal at his home where he is currently living that is breakdown of our interview

Q1 When did you know realise you were dyslexia ?
A1) *I have never been stated as being Dyslexic, my wife really thinks I am, I think I'm just bad at spelling and not confident when reading something for the first time.*

Q2 can you tell us a time in your life experience it really effect you?
A2) *I think throughout my time at school was the worst time, I never felt comfortable learning and understanding many subject, I always*

thought I wasn't as good as the other children at learning and some time would say I understood even if I didn't.

Q3 what about a time you think it help you out?
A3)*Not sure if it help or hindered me, but once I did put on a job application that I may be slightly dyslexic, I think it may have been a job for a Local Authorities, if it had been for a corporate company I would not have mentioned it.*

Q4 any silly funny story that you think feel dyslexia contributed to it?
A4) *I used to deliver a number of course where I would have to facilitate people into groups to participate in the workshops, I would have to write things up on a flip chart etc, and I would always make references to my bad spelling, and that there was no need for the candidates doing writing for the group to worry about any spelling mistakes.*

Q5 any routine, habits, tactics you use to overcome day to day tasks?
A5) *I have always tried to plan my work in advance so that I can cover any event, but of course this is not possible, so when thinks happen out of the out of the blues this causes me a problem and all me fears come into play.*

Q6 If the 12-year-old you came up and ask you for advice what would you tell them?
A6) *To believe in your self you can achieve anything in life if your*

prepared to work hard and look a various ways and strategies to learn.

Q7 if you could put in or change something in the special needs education system what would you implement to help develop young people with dyslexia?
A7 *Every primary schoo l to have a specialist dyslexic unit/teacher that would work with all children perceived to have some form of dyslexia.*

Q8 as a parent what or with not child or children with dyslexia what advice would you give?
A8) *Seek alternative ways to support your child, all children learn in different ways, try to get your child to a school who have an open mind about learning.*

Q9 if you had a choice, who would you like to be for one day?
A9) *Rodger Federer. Absolutely sheer class.*

Q10 who was you role model idle growing up ?
A10) *My PE Teacher at secondary school Mr Richards gave me so much confidence in sport, which in turn gave me my confidence in life, making friends, being part of teams, being admired by other.*

Hope that helps Andy,

Thank you so much Larry for doing this!

OWLS LOTTE

Ian Denmen former firefighter, UKBFF bodybuilding champion, owns a building construction company and friend

I used speech pad for this interview and I honestly believe it's a great way to get ideas and information down if your writing a book ha-ha or an essay paper you simple dictate on your phone or record as I did and send it off it cost me £11 which is worth the money for this so below is us

AW = Me/Interviewer
ID = Ian /Interviewee

AW : So I'll just start on this. with Ian Denmen today - first question would be, when did you realize Lloyd had dyslexia

Interviewee: *Yeah, it's all about my son, Lloyd, who is now 32. When did we first realize? I guess I think it was as late on as about eight or nine years old, I think. It certainly wasn't an early detection, because he had many behavioural problems. And it was just put down as bad behaviour. So it was one teacher. I can't remember who it was, but there was one teacher who actually spotted that he was dyslexic. And then when we started reading into dyslexia, getting books on it, because there was no internet at the time, then we found out that a lot of his tantrums, and the way he behaved, and his bad behaviour problems was all part of his dyslexia. He's frustrated because he's not understanding, etc.*

Interviewer: Yeah, my thing was similar with my mom and dad. Because I remember when they said to my mom and dad, they were like, "Oh, we think he's got ADHD."

Interviewee: *Exactly that. He got...he had seen the school psychiatric nurse and they were banging about ADHD. But I mean I'll go and pick him up from school, and he would come running over to us, launch his bag, kick me in the shins, and just walk straight past me. And then it turns out later on, that was part of his dyslexia. Having had eight hours with people that he can't communicate with, his pent up frustration, and then take it straight on the first person that he knows he can do it and get away with.*

Interviewer: Yeah, no, that's hard to take !

Interviewee: *And that was an acquired inherent behaviour of his dyslexia, that people that love him unconditionally that he can get away with, then he can launch out and kick and then he'd be all right after that initial first kick in the shin.*

Interviewer: Yeah, you were his stress relief, isn't it?

Interviewee: *Yeah, stress relief, yeah, that's it. And he'd say, "I didn't have a good day." Wham, bang. And I'd say, "Oh, I didn't have a good day then." And then he'd be fine after that.*

Interviewer: Yeah, I found that with football. I literally... I hated school. Literally, struggled, bullied people, just the whole, like he said, eight hours of going, "What am I doing here?" I have no idea what's going on. And then all of a sudden, I'd see my parents, and then they'd be like, "Why are you so quiet?" And then all of a sudden, the only time I enjoyed things was when I was going home at 4:00, to go play football at 5:00. That was because it was obviously a really stressful day. Which leads on to question number two. Can you tell us a time in your life experience it really affected you?

Interviewee : *Well taking a kick in the shin, so that affected me, yeah, about a quarter to 4:00 every day, usually to be honest.*

Interviewer: Mr. Shins.

Interviewee: *Yeah, not just that, obviously a bit of worry in them early years when he was detected, thinking you've got an unruly kid. And the stigma that was gonna be attached to him because he was a naughty boy all the time, always getting dug out. And then yeah, thinking, especially Alex more than me, really sad that you'd have to go through all that because no one fucking diagnosed or spotted that he was dyslexia.*

Interviewer: Do you think it affect you or your family because obviously Carly hasn't got it. But then with you and Alex, do you think it affected anything relationship wise with kind of behaviour?

Interviewee: *No, I don't think so.*

Interviewer: No?

Interviewee: *No, I can't say it was so stressful that it was like family disruptive, no. I don't think so.*

Interviewer: So the next one would be, what about a time you think that it helped you or with obviously, Lloyd, helped Lloyd within his career or growing up?

Interviewee: *Yeah, I guess I think it's helped him out a little bit leaving school. Because one thing he was really worried about was not getting a job, which is pretty much why I started the firm and put in for his for apprenticeship in bricklaying.*

Interviewee: *I started that firm, the whole reason was to give Lloyd a job, because he was worried about not having a job. So I mean I was glad to be just building on my days off, because I was already in the fire service. But then obviously, I saw an opportunity, I liked the challenge. But also I thought if I can get something going, I could take Lloyd on as soon as he left school. So I did. So I started a firm about a year before he left school, and always, "Don't you worry. You can work with me." And it made him a lot happier knowing he's got a job when he leaves school.*

Interviewer: And obviously it's led onto what he's doing now.

Interviewee: *Yeah, Definitely I think his dyslexia, it helped him out, is that he's kind of excelled in pretty much everything else he's ever done. Obviously the way his brain works, he's very meticulous with everything else he does, which doesn't involved writing and reading.*

Interviewer: Yeah, and do you think that's good with obviously even yourself, painting pictures and seeing the bigger picture like drawings and kind of seeing patterns up obviously with brickwork and construction, actually physically?

Interviewee: *Yeah, I think he's definitely...he was a very good brick-layer. He does insulating now. But I think he's done really well. He's doing really well. He seems to have his life in order, that's for sure.*

Interviewer: so for you, that he's done well and achieved well.

Interviewee: *Yeah, definitely, yeah, definitely. I mean he would have carried on probably bricklaying if it wasn't for the 2008 recession all the fucking bankers caused. But that's another story. But he probably would have bricklaying, and not have to go into insulating. Basically, his mate, Joe Burns , had a job with his...gone off the building onto insulating. Because he was with the girl whose dad owned the whole big company. So he said to Lloyd, "I can get you work." Because the bricklaying, the whole building work just shut down over night in 2008. And I said to Lloyd, "Go with him if he's got work. Don't hang about on the building." Which he did, and he's never looked back really. Never come back on the building, which is good.*

Interviewer: And then with you, you've obviously been a building also yourself and bricklaying. When you obviously see him doing the work, were you proud? But at the same time, kind of a thing that you're thinking how he picked up so quickly?

Interviewee: *Yeah, just also just really noticing the difference between his confidence in what he was doing that than his confidence he was ever doing anything that involved literacy at school, whatever. I mean he would avoid going out for meals, because he knew it meant reading the menu. We didn't treat that till quite a long time. He would always kick off and make an excuse why he didn't wanna come. And then he tweaked out, it was because there was gonna be a menu and he didn't wanna have to read it. But yeah, obviously it's all like the difference in his attitude towards, and his skill level was so much far above than when he had to sit in the classroom with books and pens.*

Interviewer: Yeah, amazing. The same thing, when you say that, I remember freaking out. If I had to go to a restaurant, if it had numbers, that was all right. If they had a restaurant list, I'd go, "Oh, I want number seven."

Interviewee: *Number seven, yeah.*

Interviewer: Number twelve, it was such a big list.

Interviewee: *Yeah, but you didn't have that. Yeah, exactly that, yeah. It's a copout, yeah. So I can see that.*

Interviewer: Yeah, and question four. Any silly, funny stories that you think or feel dyslexia contributed to? So obviously things that Lloyd had done, or things that you think in a way, because of the way he works, or the way his brain functions and... Because from when I see him, he's always a comedian,

Interviewee: *Lloyd's a character. He's still a comedian. Whether dyslexia has contributed to it or not, I don't know. I couldn't really specifically say anything that dyslexia attributed to. He's definitely a comedian and he still is.*

Interviewer: Yeah, I remember.

Interviewee: *He's a whiskey drinking comedian got into drinking whiskey and he's like I said, "Oh, I nearly you a bottle the other day. It was Jack Daniels. Not normal." And he goes, "Oh, that would be Gentleman Jack." He said it's slightly different exposure in a different way, and curated. And then Lloyd would go in to tell me exactly everything he's done from start to finish, and we made up.*

Interviewer: He's not addicted, but it's once he gets into something, he's 100%

Interviewee: *I said, "Yeah, my friend is into whiskeys." I said, "I watched a documentary on a country that you wouldn't imagine that made whiskeys, but they reckon better than Scotland." He goes, "Oh, that's Japan, because Japan now makes it." And then he goes off again. Fuck, you know, but that's just the way his brain his.*

Interviewee: *Good communicators, yeah.*

Interviewer: And that's why a lot of comedians a lot of these people have got dyslexia.

Interviewee: *Oh, yeah, he's very confident, very loud. Yeah, he's flat out comedian, yeah, for sure. Even more so now. Now he's old enough to consume alcohol. Yeah, definitely.*

Interviewer: Oh, brilliant. So next question. Any routine tactics you use to overcome day to day tasks?

Interviewee: *Yeah, well first, it's for you. It's that thing that you've got in the routine for obviously for exercise and people for the book, is kind of...is there things that you've got that literally stuck in your whole kind of...it's even automatic to you. But to someone whose never exercised, or someone that's gotta get off their ass and basically*

Interviewer: For me, now personally?

Interviewee: *Yeah.*

Interviewer: Is there things in your day to day tasks, routines? So things that might be, you get up at this time, and you have a coffee, and get on a bike, go to the beach?

Interviewee: *Yeah, let me think. Everything is a routine, isn't it? You know what it's like, the bodybuilding diets. Even though you're not competing, you still do it, yeah. Everything's absolutely routine. Food, training, always is.*

Interviewer: What's that like with work, in the sense... Is there things you go, "Right, the first thing I do in the morning before

I go to work, I do this. When I get on site..." Or even when you were at the fire service, things as soon as you got in. Is there something that you feel, even today, you go, "Right, as soon as I do that..." Anytime in the day, there's something that you think that a routine that's carried you through your life sort of thing? Yeah, even in your struggles. Things you tell me you think, you know, if you're having a bad time or a good time. There's something that's always there that you think that's for Ian, as a person?

Interviewee: *Yes, just getting in the gym, I guess. That's the only main constant through my life. The other things have come and gone, yeah. I've always gone to the gym, no matter what I'd still go to the gym and the other end of the spectrum, when I'm really happy I'll go to the gym real lot, but I've always gone to the gym. I've not always eaten that healthy, but I'll still go to the gym.*

Interviewer: Yeah, so that's your fundamental...

Interviewee: *Yeah, that is...yeah, if I don't go to the gym, I'm in trouble. If I'm not going to the gym, if I've given up going to the gym, then I'm in a bad place.*

Interviewer: Right, okay.

Interviewee: *Definitely. Yeah, I've only ever done that... Well I've never done it. I've never done it through problems. I've done it through injury, like now. I've done it when I've had operations and stuff, I'll stop going to the gym. But I've never done it through lifestyle change ever.*

Interviewer: Oh, okay.

Interviewee: *I've come close a few times, but I've always managed to drag my ass to the gym. I think if I didn't manage to go, if I wasn't going to the gym, I would be either seriously depressed or in a bad place, for sure.*

Interviewer: So even in any kind of aspect, you've just gone, "Do you know what? I'll get off my ass. I'm going to the gym."

Interviewee: *Always, always, whether I've been getting divorced, whether I've been battling fucking alcohol or whatever, I always go to the gym. Always, even if I've been training on the fire service training school at a new job, I'd find a gym. I'd always go, for sure. I've had a few bad accidents and well, I have been out, got to the gym for a few months. But that's just the way it is. Any routine, habits, tactics used to overcome day to day tasks.*

Interviewer: So now it would be, if a 12-year-old came up to you and asked you for advice, what would you tell them? So the 12-year-old you knew, or even if a bit older. Say even a 15 or 16-year-old who has come out of school, what would you then... Even if it's one big thing that you'd go, "You know what? I'll tell that kid, so when he gets older, he's always got something..."

Interviewee: *Yeah, I'm just trying to think. It's a tough one, isn't it? It's a tough. I mean you could do a specific like, don't get married before your 25, or you could do a specific like, don't take drugs. But I don't think any of that's really relevant. I guess just do what you want, really, isn't it?*

Interviewer: Just do what you want with your life.

Interviewee: *Do what you want. Do what you want, yeah, I guess is the answer to that one.*

Interviewer: Yeah, so obviously, that a 15, 16-year-old...what was you like at 15 or 16?

Interviewee: *I did what made me happy, I absolutely did. I didn't really take any exams and didn't really do a lot. Didn't really find myself until I was 18.*

Interviewer: And was that with the gym when you was 18?

Interviewee: *No, I found Alex and got married. And that I had to work. I had to work because I had to buy a house*

Interviewer: So a bit of a hurricane.

Interviewee: *Yeah, that's another story, yeah. Yeah, so I supposed I had to grow up. That's all right.*

Interviewer: Yeah, so if you could change in the special needs education system, what would you implement? I

Interviewee : *I would just have to pass on that, because I don't have anything to do with the special needs system. It doesn't affect my life right now, and if you had asked me that question maybe 25 years ago when Lloyd was at school, I'd probably have a whole bundle of answers for you.*

Interviewer: Yeah, no, that's all right. No, it's just obviously for me, because it's just kind of things to help. Because obviously, my mum and dad, I've found it hard.

Interviewee: *Okay, yeah, there is one thing I'll do to change. This is not a joke answer, it's a true answer. The special needs education is all stuck, Right, i.e., Brexit. Get out of EU. Until such time that the failing governments would pour money into the infrastructure to create a system that can cope with the problems that we've got. Because these problems are only gonna be escalated right across the board. All the time, we've been failed by these corrupt governments that have just been, for years and years, let more and more people to get their tax money and their revenue to boost the economy. And then they just fail us on pouring it back into the infrastructure. And that's fact.*

Interviewer: Yeah, and schools, and hospitals, yeah.

Interviewee: *I mean you've got class sizes of 35-plus, multinationals, and everything is too stretched. So how on earth are you gonna learn? What was the question? (question repeated) How on earth are you ever gonna do something for the special needs, when you can't even afford to deal with normal students? Which are not causing you extra work.*

Interviewee: *That's not a racist answer. I'm all for multi cultures, I'm all for governments. Do you know what I mean? If you want another 500 people in your business, then put at least a few more chairs in the staff room. You know what I mean?*

Interviewer: Yeah, spot on, yeah.

Interviewee: *Which is what's been going wrong in this country.*

Interviewer: With a child with dyslexia, what advice would you give? So obviously, having Lloyd, but of course you've got both. But just kind of for parents who just have found out basically. Because they're gonna have no idea, even today. They're gonna just be told that their kid's done a test, and they are dyslexic

Interviewee: *Yeah. What advice would I give? I think just what we've done really. I mean it's easier now with the access to information on internet to find out. I mean the first thing we had done was went and bought a book on it, and just sort of like, yeah, equip yourself, everything you can find out about it that will help you understand what's going on. That's probably the best bit of advice. Now you just hit Google, don't you?*

Interviewer: Yeah. Do you find not that you changed. But then when you found out, obviously because of Lloyd kicking your shins and kind of you thinking he's a naughty kid when he's not. He's just frustrated. Do you feel that you've changed as a parent towards him?

Interviewee: *Absolutely, 100%, yeah.*

Interviewer: And what do you think you've changed most about you in the sense of when you found out?

Interviewee: *Just a lot more tolerance, and a lot more of, yeah, just tolerance. A lot more understanding, and also just trying to work with him on his literacy disabilities, so that he could like...you know, to try and help to overcome it or to at least reach a better level. And yeah, and also siblings as well. Like his sister, she was pretty good, educating her about it.*

Interviewer: So if you've got brothers and sisters, it's good for them to get involved?

Interviewee: *Absolutely, yeah, absolutely, yeah. To create a more tolerant environment, yeah, for sure.*

Interviewer: And I'll say, I didn't know that. You've built a whole business basically from that.

Interviewee: *Built a business, yeah, really my motivation was to give Lloyd a job, yeah. It lasted 10 years.*

Interviewer: But yeah, but that's huge. That's a good message.

Interviewee: *Yeah, it was a good thing to come out of it. And it gave Lloyd a good start in life as well. Give him...he was a really good bricklayer. He's never laid a brick in years now, but he was really good.*

Interviewer: So Julia Roberts, I'll put in there that you wanna be Julia Roberts for the day. No, I'm joking.

Interviewee: *If you had a choice, who would you like to be? Yeah, whoever is banging Julia Roberts. It's quite easy. Or yeah, whoever is banging Victoria Pendleton. Probably Pendleton, actually. Who was your role model, idol growing up? It probably would have been someone who was around when I was growing up?*

Interviewer: Yeah, so like it could be someone that's influenced you when you were younger. It could be someone that when you were training that you talked to.

Interviewee: *Yeah, it would have just been probably muscle man in one of my dad's muscle magazines probably, growing up.*

Interviewer: Oh, so what muscle magazine?

Interviewee: *Oh, God knows. Whatever it was back in the day. My dad had a few muscle magazines. This was before the time anything was on TV, and I used to look for it in muscle magazines. That's what I al used to look for it in muscle magazines. That's what I always wanted to do. I always wanted to do it, right from the age of about 10, 11. I can remember that. Yeah. And then watching "Pumping Iron." "Pumping Iron" came out on TV in 1976, I think it come out on TV. There was a documentary "Pumping Iron," '76 or '77. I think I was about 12 then. And I sat in front of it and watched "Pumping Iron" with my dad. And then that was it. That was my direction in life, for sure. I remember it come on channel four. Shortly after channel four after come onto air because there was only three channels. And there was the launching of channel four, and then that was one of the new channel four documentaries, "Pumping Iron." Me and my dad sat and watched it.*

Interviewer: And that was it, you just fell in to it?

Interviewee: That was it, yeah.

Interviewer: *See, I always remember mine. I started to obviously... From a young age, but I still see...come around your house all the time. Obviously, it's been there. And then I've seen "London Burning," I used to always watch on. I always wanted to be a firefighter. And then I would see is one. And then I used to see you train, and you come home in your track suit or shell suit.*

Interviewee: Shell suit, yeah.

Interviewer: But I remember I said to my mum and dad, I was like, "I wanna be a fireman. And I wanna train." So then my mom and dad bought these Yorkie weights, they had sand in it.

Interviewee: *Yeah, similar to the ones I've got yeah.*

Interviewer: Yeah, but my room was the tiniest room. So I remember sticking on a "Rocky" CD, the music from the film. I remember I used to stick it...I had a tape one. And put it in, and I remember I was sitting and I would start training on my bed, or doing deadlifts or something. Obviously break everything in my room. But I remember one day, I was coming down with you, and I think that's when it hit. And I put it in the book. But I was 14, and I'd come on work experience at a station.

Interviewer: And you coming down, you go, "Right, we're gonna do a fitness test." And I remember being there with you, and you went, "Right, if you pass all this, you would pass getting in."

Interviewee: *Getting in, yeah.*

Interviewer: And I remember, all of a sudden, I just knew it was something I had to. Because I never had to think about it in terms of tests but I had support. I remember you used to love shouting at me. I remember you used to be like, "You've got to do 10 reps. If you can do 60 kilos at that age you will pass" I remember being in the BA in the rat run . And you was like, "Well if you don't do this, that person's not gonna survive." them kind of things. I found I loved it and wanted to do it. I obviously got there eventually, in kind of a different way. So I'm playing football. I love football. I've gotta get stronger. If I'm gonna be a good footballer, I've gotta get fitter, and I've got to be physically fit (im 15 at this time) because I wasn't big but then I had a growth spurt. I wasn't the tallest or biggest. But then I was becoming a bean pole with no muscles. So I think that was for me, was the moment I fell in love with fitness and the gym you motivated me. Because to me, as I said to you before, but when you're younger and you have someone you look up to, and you go, "he's like a he-man to me. I was like, "I like he-man. So I wanna be a he-man." Do you know what I mean?

So you had muscle magazines and obviously "Pumping Iron" was there.

Interviewee: *Yeah, I don't feel like there was any one figure around me that was my role model. I mean I used to look up to my dad a lot, because my dad always cycling. My dad, he always lifted weights. And I remember I was a real tiny little kid. I used to think he was just fucking huge. He used to say to make him show us his biceps and we used to hang off his arms as kids. And I used to think he was to all my little mates used to say, "Your dad's massive." Looking back, I suppose he used to have 16-inch arms. But that was before. He was like fucking enormous. He used to have this bicep like that.*

So yeah, I suppose as a really age, yeah, I suppose my dad was my role model. But then he used to show me pictures of blokes that were fucking huge. And I would think, fucking hell. And then you realize that there's a lot of life outside of the four walls.

Interviewer: Oh, yeah, no. And the last thing, obviously I'm going into another chapter, would be, is there kind of one or two tips for someone whose never basically done exercise before? So this would be the first one, is kind of fundamentally, you think are massively important for them to start? And also then one thing, kind of someone whose got into the gym, and who's really kinda then pushing themselves, and kind of wanting to progress maybe into bodybuilding or into just a lifestyle of just having it. What kind of free fundamental kind of tips or principles do you think?

Interviewee: *I think the first thing, the most important thing is to always set yourself goals, which are attainable. Whether that's whether you're first starting off or whether you're getting more into it, is to... You know what I mean? If you're someone that's never been at a gym before, never done exercise, don't set your schedule five...you know, a 20-minute run every morning and three times a night in the gym.*

Because you'll fail about week one. So you've always gotta set yourself targets which are attainable. And I still do that now. If I'm actually fucked coming off a building site, but I don't wanna miss my workout, I will set myself a workout in my head, which is short, fast and furious. And I know I can do it. Be in and be out in 20 minutes. So I still do it now.

And I think that's really important for all levels to set yourself, like, if you're moving up a scale making fitness and nutrition your lifestyle, don't bite off more than you can chew. Because you won't achievement. You get despondent and it's really important to feel like you're achieving what you set yourself out. Just gradual increases in your intensity and all the rest of it, so you can carry on achieving what you set out. I think that's really important.

Interviewer: Oh, good. And then probably last, for someone who is really... Like, for me, I've found that when I was with you, I found that when I was at kind of points of struggling, obviously because I wanted to do it for me, personally, and for Harry, and obviously for you. They were the three kinda triangles of keeping me going. At the same time, I found that for me, I'd like to picture at the end, the final thing?

Interviewee: *Yeah, that's good to always to have the visualization of where you wanna get. But even when we had done you, we didn't set a diet week to week with unattainable goals. It was like a pound a week or whatever. Do you know what I mean? We give ourselves to here, and we should have hit five pound gone. So again, that's all about just making it achievable and not beating yourself up too much if you don't do it, but cracking on. Success comes from not giving up, doesn't it? Not from anything else, really. The same as...yeah, if you slip up on your diet, then get back on it the next day. If you give up and think, oh, I didn't try, then you're back where you started.*

Interviewer: Yeah. That's it, mate.

Interviewee: *Yeah, that was good. That was good fun, mate.*

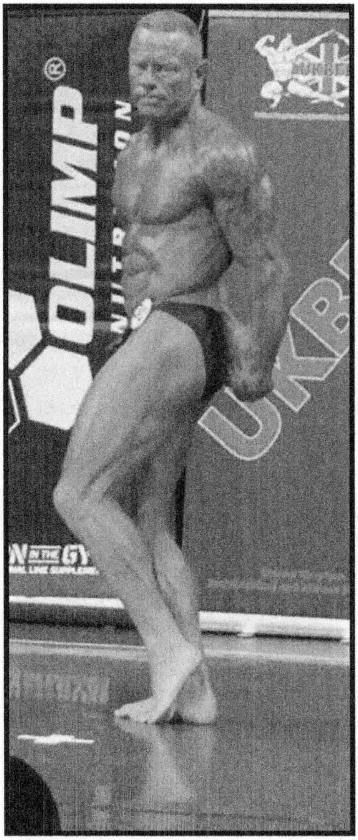

Daniel Petch

living in Australia and working as a electrical engineer achieving great things and most important my nephew as well

Q1 when did you know realise you were dyslexia

When I was in First School, unsure what year, but I noticed I was not doing the same things as the other children. I used to play boardgames with the teacher's assistant.

Q2 can you tell us a time in your life experience it really effect you

Not until recently, in my current role and starting my adult apprenticeship as an Electrician. Before now, my previous roles were hands on.

Q3 what about a time you think it help you out

Dyslexia has never helped me as such

Q4 any silly funny story that you think feel dyslexia contributed to it

My wife purchased a very large bookcase for our house, which I was unaware of at the time, when I came home from being away at work, it was filled to the brim with books. I said 'well these are all useless as I have never read a book in my life'

Q5 any routine, habits, tactics you use to overcome day to day tasks

My phone helps me write emails and texts, I speak into the phone and it writes out what I am saying (there is a feature on the phone for this, still not always a 100% sure if its correct)

Using Spellcheck on emails

Remembering words through reading and writing with my apprenticeship

Q6 if the 12-year-old you, came up and ask you for advice what would you tell them ?

Reading is key and as hard as it is, you need to persevere with it. Do not give up on reading. I believe reading is key. Learn certain techniques which work for you. Try not to be disheartened when you get something wrong and always ask for help and don't be afraid to ask for the help.

Q7 if you could put in or change something in the special needs education system what would you implement to help develop young people with dyslexia.

When I was younger, dyslexia wasn't common and I don't believe teachers or the education system knew how to manage or deal with kids with dyslexia. I would hope now, the education system is more aware and knowledgeable and have the skills and tools to help and bring out the best in the kids and adults who continue to find learning challenging.

Q8 as a parent who or with not child or children with dyslexia what advice would you give.

Same answer as Q6

Q9 if you had a choice who would you like to be for one day?

My grandad his a funny man

Q10 who was you role model growing up ?

I have always looked up to my dad, I have always admired his work ethics.

Conclusion:

So after this journey we have been on together I hope that I made you cry, made you laugh and I hope I've made you take action now. I will leave you with my version of Kipling – "who do you think you are, you've written a book now your fucking Kipling!"

If you ever met me or want to speak to me just contact me in chapter 10 ,

If you think you won't amount to much then your are wrong ,

If in the early days you are finding it tough then don't panic you know your brain works a different way and you are a machines with a gift

If you start failing again then your on the road to success

If you pick up a barbell or find your own Jim and start working harder them those around you then your mind-set will change and become stronger and your strength will improve.,

If you remove your old habit and tools and replace them with your new tactics and skills if you can aim for your dreams and fall short then pick up again with all your knowledge

If after all this to reached the next stage then find a coach or coach others and with every bit of knowledge you receive or pass then the world well be your oyster and everything in it and which is more than you can imagine.

You're dyslexic my friend –Congratulations!

USEFUL LINKS AND RESOURCES

British Dyslexia Association

Unit 6a Bracknell beeches

Old Bracknell lane Bracknell RG12 7BW

SPEECHPAD

Transcription by Speechpad

www.speechpad.com

Support questions: support@speechpad.com

Sales questions: sales@speechpad.com

Destiny performance

Email andywebb@destinyperfomance.com

Twitter:destinyperform1

Facebook : destiny performance

The Eye Academy

49 high street Guildford GU1 3DY

Email guildford@eyeacademy.com

Made by dyslexia company

INFO@MADEBYDYSLEXIA.ORG

Learn by DYSLEXIA

OFFICE 2 THE BARNS FARM ROAD CADDSDOWN INDSTRIAL PARK

BIDEFORD NORTH DEVON EX39 3BT

TEL 07727298806

ACKNOWLEDGMENTS:

So before I go on a Joaquin Phoenix Oscar style speech go on for 14 pages, I want to thank as many people as I can, if I forgot you, I do apologise. But obviously, if I started writing about every single person, that'd be another book. So firstly with "How to Become with Richard, Jordan and Josh." They're the three people who have really helped me inspire me but also helped me publish and create this and I can't thank them enough, and we're going be doing some more work in the future together, and some more crazy plans that I have.

Then I want say thank you to the negative people, because everyone in life has people that made experience like I've done for this book, and a negative people I want say thank you. There's so many of you out there that help me get to a position where I want help as many people as I possibly can in life, and because of your things have given me the desire to push on.

Friends, there's so many friends out there that I want say thank you to. Every single one of you makes my life better and changes my life for the best. There's things I've learned so much from each individual, one of you, and you've been a part of my life has helped me be the person I am today. So I can't ever thank you enough.

So I'm going thank my big sister, the bookend, so she's the oldest, I'm the youngest. And we keep all the craziness in the middle is what we believe. And what I want do is thank you for inspiring me and the fact that you've got your own business. For of being one of my biggest cheerleaders. I come to you sometimes and I'll talk about an idea or something I want do, and you kind of give me the green light and you tell me the truth, which is massively important. And for that, I'll always thank you.

And I hope that you'll be on more of my adventures in the future.

Then I want thank my big brother Roy. He's the Robinson Crusoe of this family. So Roy's given me the skill and inspired me and watching him over the years just go off and do what he wants. He's travelled the world, he's been to some amazing places. He's lived all these different little lives. And for me, it gave me the kind of sense to go out there and go for it. Doesn't really matter what people think. And he has given me that kind of thing which I put in the book. So I just want say I love you and thank you big brother.

To my sister, Karen, I want to thank you for being that sister that has always been there for me from the ups and downs. There's always been time's where you get to a point in life and there's always someone next to you there. And you've always been that person in some aspects. And I want thank you for that. And obviously, you've been what I've put in the book before. But for you as well, I just hope you find your gift and your happiness because you have so much more to give to the world. And I believe one day you'll find that and a lot of people will realise and know how talented you are.

My nieces and nephews, so Daniel, Jade, Stephen, and David, you've given me things that as an uncle, I took responsibility on from a young age, even though one of you is older than me. But we've stayed friends, which is massively important life. And for all of you, I just want you to know how proud I am of you for the lives that you've now achieved and taken on. And I just want you to know that wherever you are in the world, as some of you in Australia, David, you could be anywhere in the world saving the world. Steven, I'm always there for you. And I'll always be here to guide and support you in whatever you decide you want do in life. So I love you all.

My sister Lorraine, I want thank you firstly, you're the only person in the world that calls me Ange, which is hilarious. I think something massively you've given to me is from a young boy growing up into a teenager, all them parties and all the time in the summer being with you and Dave, and the family that I learned skills to talk to people and incorporate people in and how to listen and learn. And learn from you good things, learned how to do certain things, not to do certain things. And I think that is a massive thing in life when you're growing as a person. So I love you for that. I know you're in Australia, you're far away,

Now Issy wizzy. I came into your life at seven years old. And even though I'm not your dad, I love you like you're my own daughter. And something you've given to me which I'll forever be grateful for and the little stories. That one day I dropped Harry off to his mums and I was at a very low point in my life. I got to a point where dark thoughts start happening again and things that you don't want happen. I was so upset I wasn't going see Harry for a while. And as I came home, a the little voice said, "I'm coming down Andy." And wanting to show me as you always do something. As you came down with your little tiara on your head, your long sleeve princess gloves and a cape on and some butterfly wings.

And as you come down with your little fairy wonders, well, you started dancing and telling me that you were the nudey ferry. And you snapped me out of the position I was in and made me realise that whatever's going on, whatever situation or whatever I feel that every time I come home, I've got another little person to take care of. And for that I can never really thank you enough for and hopefully when you get older, maybe you'll read this book, but you'll realise just how much I love you. And hopefully as time goes on, that I will help you become the person that you want to become. So I love you very much.

My little Harry, my vision, my dream, my ambition, all comes from getting you to where you want be in life. Every person in this book has inspired me and in their own ways, but for you every time I'm with you, I'm just so happy. And I just so want create the best life for you. I hope in time, as you get older, we talk and I learn and I try and teach all the things that I can to make you the best person you can be. I hope that wherever you decide to do in life, that I'll be by your side, because I always will forever. I just want you to know that I love you so much. And as time goes by, that you will understand all the things that we do together, and you have the great life that I want try and give to you. Please, forever remember that Daddy loves you and your daddy's best friend.

Mum and Dad, wow, where do you start with this? So I just want to thank you for being the best parents I could possibly have. You've supported me you love me the most important thing. You've taught me lessons that give me the foundations to be who I am and you can't take that away from anyone. Always, muck about with you and say that you know, I'm the special one because it took you the fifth time to make a decent one, minor joke. But you've given me the fundamentals to blossom into the person I am and give me all the skills. I can never thank you enough and I hope in time that I teach my kids the same values and principles that will lead them on to a better life as you've created kind of a legacy. And, you know, dynasty as you say for a family. I could sit here all day and say certain things and how you are and what you do for me, but I don't think I could really get it all down.

Dad once said to me that when he's in gardening because I'm not a gardener, he loves gardening. He's amazing at it. But he said to me, "You gotta have good grounds, good foundation, and good environments to create amazing plants." And that's what you've given to me. I hope I feel I've blossomed and that you will be proud of me. And I know which is important for me that you're not always going be around and there's going be a time when I can't pick up the phone and ask you for advice or talk to ask how your day is. So hopefully, once you've read all this book, mum, because dad won't read it, that you understand me more. And hopefully you know, you see how much you two have influenced me. And this is the best that I could possibly do on paper

My beautiful wife to be. Firstly, there's not enough words from Shakespeare, from the Bible, from anywhere that couldn't express how much you mean to me and what you've done for me, I'd have to write another 10-15 million books I think. But a massive thing of law of attraction springs to mind. So I dreamed about having you in my life, about having this amazing perfect person and you arrived and it's not through hard work and myself, but you just do everything for me that I can't ever thank you enough for you inspire me. You fell in love with me, you think I'm amazing which is scary in itself. You put up with all my crazy adventures